MW01229701

COURAGEOUS OVERCOMERS
Anthology

Stories to uplift, comfort and inspire...

Commodore (Ret.) Tellis A. Bethel Sr., Dr. Deborah Pople-Smith, Theo O. Rolle, Brenda Dewis, Dr. Deborah Bartlett, Kaynell Gould, Lt. Commander Delvonne Duncombe, Darnella Diggis, Sherry Tyndle, Philippa Melvyn, Anna L. Lewis, Teri M. Bethel.

ISBN: 9798848367065
Publisher: Inspire Publishing, The Bahamas
www.InspirePublishing.org
Cover Design: Teri M. Bethel

DISCLAIMER

DEDICATION

To the courageous men, women, and children who refuse to stay down when knocked low...

PRIVACY

Due to the nature of some of these events, several names have been changed to protect identities.

TABLE OF CONTENTS

Anna L. Lewis

Teri M. Bethel

I learned that courage was not the absence of fear, but the triumph over it. The brave man is not he who does not feel afraid, but he who conquers that fear.

Nelson Mandella

Former President of South Africa

INTRODUCTION

It takes courage to stand amid adversity, to choose to do right when right seems difficult. It takes courage not to faint under pressure when the load seems too much for you to bear. It also takes courage to muster the strength to roar like a lion when your strength has waned. As the stories in this anthology reveal, your focus cannot be on your senses, that is, what you see or how you feel if you are to overcome adversities in life. To overcome, you must be resolute in trusting the Master's plan, the Creator's guidebook (the Holy Bible), to implement winning strategies for your life.

Courageous Overcomers is a collection of real-life stories by twelve ordinary people who have come through extraordinary situations in the Bahamas. This anthology is a voice of encouragement for those in similar circumstances wondering how others made it through. If that is you or someone you know, we encourage you to read this book and perhaps gift a copy as a small way of letting people know that they are not alone in their trials.

Others have gone before and have made it through despite the odds—you can too.

Going through dire situations can feel overwhelming. You may feel that no one would believe your story or even care. The truth is, there is probably someone somewhere prayerfully rooting for you. The way to stay trapped is by being badgered into isolation. The animal kingdom isolates its prey, and when they least expect it, they are converged upon. If life is beating you down, get help. Read the Holy Bible and ask Heaven to guide you to a confidential, trustworthy source for support. We have included a few helpful scriptures at the end of the book to comfort and strengthen you as you prepare to take your victory lap.

This book is not intended to preach, condemn or condone. We believe the stories here will encourage you to stand firm and assume the posture of victory. Like a wrestler in the ring, you need to know when to duck, when to throw a blow, and when to tag your partner. If you are a believer, then your partner is Jesus Christ. He's waiting for you to tag him. If you're not, we ask you to consider it. After all, the word of God says that the thief has come to kill, steal, and destroy, but the Lord has come to give you an abundant life. Will you choose to tag him? Your freedom can begin today.

BEYOND THE WILD SIDE

Commodore (Ret.) Tellis A. Bethel Sr.

Bethel! Bethel! Bethel!" Lieutenant Jackson Ritchie, my commanding officer (CO), screamed above the piercing noise of machine-gun fire. It was shortly after midnight. I was below the deck of a large barge with my boarding team. We were searching a Bahamian barge for drugs when shots rang out above. HMBS Inagua was completing its patrol when we received an intelligence report concerning a mother ship with drugs aboard near Hole-in-the-Wall at the southern end of Abaco.

I was the ship's boarding officer and was second in command of HMBS Inagua. It was shortly after midnight, and we were wrapping up the search without finding any drugs aboard. That's when Lt. Ritchie shouted my name. The boarding team and I ran up the stairs only to see the sky lit up with red tracer shots from Inagua's machine gun firing into the dark of night. After returning to Inagua, Lt. Ritchie quickly pointed in the direction of the tracer shots at a vessel that had just tried to ram our boat. It was the mother ship we were looking for earlier. The 80-foot Colombian vessel came to transfer its huge cargo of drugs to the Bahamian barge. Inagua had arrived a little too early. The unlit vessel's silhouette could barely be seen. Lt. Ritchie ordered me, Able Seamen Andrew Hamilton, and Ricky Sealy to board the vessel. As we were preparing to jump aboard the boat, he instructed us to arrest the men hiding and secure the ship. Inagua then pulled off to give chase to a second vessel that was escorting the mother ship.

It had been a busy, rigorous morning but well worth our effort. We arrested about thirteen Colombians with over 700 bales of marijuana aboard their boat, retrieved a Colombian from the shark-infested waters, and another who was shot in the arm during the incident and caught the second vessel that tried to escape.

L-R: Acting Sub Lieutenant Tellis Bethel (age 20) Colombian prisoner, Marine Seamen Andrew Hamilton and Ricky Sealy.

The year was 1982; it was my first year on the frontline at sea. The action-packed event was one of the numerous maritime operations the Inagua crew had experienced during the peak years of the drug trade. That was life on the waters of the Bahamas. We patrolled our waters with pride to safeguard the nation while many remained unaware of what was happening within our maritime borders. In the larger scheme of things, we were mere specks on the sea, but we had a purpose and were prepared to relentlessly "Guard Our Heritage."

My Father's Influence

Those early years as a naval officer in the Royal Bahamas Defence Force were a stark contrast to my youth. For the most part, my life was meaningless; my vision was to be like my dad, Tellis Alonzo Bethel—a man who in my eyes, was larger than life. He was Sir TAB, having been knighted by a friend in a local bar. Dad was a lover, an entertainer and poet, and the man who could drink any of his bar mates under a table. Upon leaving any drinking establishment, his byline was a glass of rum for the road, with the police as the chaser. He was my hero, and I adopted his habits very early.

Lourey and Tellis Alonzo Bethel

Dad kept me and my two brothers close to him on weekends, teaching us the tricks of the trade. We learned how to drink and how to chase women. He had a way of approaching women and captivating their attention with the best lines. On one occasion, I saw him look a lady in her eyes and, with the most romantic voice, say, "One look at you, and I was lifted as by a tidal wave to the foamy crests of love and ecstasy." Her heart melted after hearing those words. Well, one day, with just him and me in the car, Dad pulled to the side of the road with urgency and, in true form, leaned over and forcefully flung my door open, shouting with mischievous enthusiasm, "Sic 'em, boy! Sic 'em." We laughed, but the young ladies ran away terrified.

I don't think the drinking pulled me in; it was Dad's charisma. He had a way of endearing people to him, especially when he belted out songs in his melodic operatic voice. His friends called him Mario Lanza, after the great American opera singer. Dad left school at fourteen to help his father support their large family. He worked himself through the ranks at the Bahamas Telecommunications Corporation, beginning as a telegraphist (Morse code operator) and eventually becoming a model manager. He was a natural comedian who made many laugh. I always admired Dad's work ethic. He was always one of the first on the job, and even though he was a manager, he was not afraid to roll his sleeve and do the dirty work himself.

Though Dad appeared to be the happy family man on the outside, our home life was difficult. Our mom Lourey (Dean) Bethel was a typical island girl who wanted nothing more than to have a loving family. Her mother died when Mom was seven, so she lived with her aunt, who raised her with her family. Life was hard for her and her two siblings (of the same parents). Mom didn't see much of her father back then, who was a Roses Long Island man. She constantly warned her sons not to have outside children reminding us that she was "a bastard," a common term used in those days for a child born out of wedlock. It was clear to my siblings and me that all Mom wanted to do was to love Dad, but his drinking habits and abusive behavior were getting the best of him. Many a weekend, we heard Mom crying when Dad got in a drunken stupor, which almost always led to him physically abusing her. Unfortunately,

Mom was not alone in this dilemma. Several of our neighbor's wives were going through the same experiences, suffering quietly in their homes.

Spending summer breaks in the Family Islands was one bright spot in those dark days. I enjoyed those happy-go-lucky days on Long Island with my cousins. Island life was a striking contrast to life in New Providence. I also had the opportunity to spend summers in Eleuthera, Grand Bahama, Rum Cay, and Abaco with relatives and friends of the family. From the moment the plane landed, I realized I was in another world. My cousins in Long Island taught me how to fish, make slingshots, hunt birds, and every other thing island boys did.

Their father, Uncle Ormand, and his wife, Aunt Patsy, my mom's sister, were hardworking people living off their farm. I remember quite clearly Aunt Patsy making what we called island bread and ironing with a gooseneck iron heated by an outside fire. I was so used to seeing Mom go to the grocery store in Nassau that I had taken it for granted how we got the food or where it came from. I also remember being awakened before dawn to watch Uncle Ormand slaughter a pig. After tying its legs, Uncle Ormand shot the pig between his eyes, cut its throat for the blood to drain, and within hours he had dehaired and portioned the meat for our meals and to share with neighbors. Those were some of the most amazing days of my life. I came to see the beauty of our country and fell in love with our waters.

The Age of Rebellion

However, the sad day came when Dad called Mom and told her to pack up and be out of the house with the children before he returned home. Not knowing what else Dad might do, Mom bundled us up and left the home they had built together. Mom grieved—now she was not only an illegitimate child but also a divorcee moving from place to place trying to keep her children together. Though petite, Mom was a strong and resilient woman who was determined to see us succeed in life. Much of the challenges she faced and overcame as a single parent were probably due to her tough upbringing on Long Island. Amazingly, she always saw the positive side of life's circumstances. However,

7

the stress and strain of life would begin to affect her later in life.

I was the second of three sons. My sister was the youngest of the four of us. Me and my two brothers were fast becoming teenage rebels not long after our folks separated. We had little supervision on the home front. Mom did what she could between work and home to keep us in check, even using the "switch" on us. What positive values she had instilled in the boys, Dad would uproot them whenever we spent time with him on weekends at the bar.

We kept all the wrong company and eventually graduated from being negatively influenced by other friends to becoming negative influencers.

Mom could do nothing to rein us in, and our dad was no help keeping his sons on the right path. We were already on the fast track to becoming alcoholics, womanizers, and party-goers, something Mom wanted us to stay clear of. It wasn't long after our parents separated that I felt the need to work to help Mom with the bills—I was twelve years old when I started working. My first summer job brought in a whopping twenty dollars working from 7 a.m. to 3 p.m. six days per week at Nassau Airport Caterers during the early 70s. I happily handed over my earnings to help Mom out with the bills. I worked in numerous trainee or line staff positions, including jobs at BATELCO, Coca-Cola, and as a bell boy on a cruise ship. My wages increased over the years, allowing me to be more supportive of the family's needs.

During the week, I spent my time helping Mom out around the home, mowing the lawn, painting portions of the house, combing my little sister's hair for school, and going to school. As time went on, I gradually developed a drinking habit. By the time I was 14, I had enjoyed getting drunk on weekends. Not long after entering tenth grade at Saint John's College, my grades began dropping.

L-R: Tellis (Andy), Kevin, Bryant and Barbara (Baubie)

I also added falling in love and crashing parties on weekends to my nefarious portfolio. In short, I practiced the art of being an angel by day and a devil at night. One day, a tenth-grade teacher at St. John's College, Mr. Yearwood, pulled me aside and told me I could be a better version of myself if I would stop "playing the fool." It was straight talk, and I knew he was right. Although I continued for several more years, Mr. Yearwood's words never wore off.

Meanwhile, I stayed on the path of being like Dad—the life of the party. One evening while with friends at a party at a Paradise Island hotel, inebriated with rum, I climbed over an upper-level railing and began swinging. I was so intoxicated that I thought I could fly like a bird and was about to try. Just before trying to do so, my younger brother grabbed me and pulled me back over the railing.

Running With the Old Boys

My part-time jobs took me around older guys whose mission was to have me engage in all vices—sex, dope, rum, fights, partying, and gambling (shooting dice). The Dance Hall at Milley's on the eastern end of town was a favorite hangout. One evening, a party we crashed soured when a young man threatened to "blow my head off." He didn't like the way I had parked my vehicle behind his. My friends decided to take the matter into their own hands. I was drunk, so I didn't take the threat seriously. Before I knew it, rocks and bottles were flying overhead; boys flew past me with dropkicks like in the movies. When the poor guy who had insulted me was on the ground unconscious, my friends fled, leaving me behind. Two days later, when I showed up to work, I was told the police wanted me to come in for questioning. I went in and answered their questions in the vaguest manner I could, not wanting to implicate my friends. I was in the hot seat, and my friends were nowhere to be found. Thankfully, the gentleman recovered. That incident was the beginning of common sense coming upon me. I could hear my mother's voice and the teacher who told me I could do better, but there was an even stronger voice on the inside, drawing me to revisit my life.

I had made all the wrong decisions drawing from the lessons I had learned from my father, apart from his work ethic. I finally realized that the father figure I always wanted and needed was not my earthly father but my heavenly Father.

A cousin invited me to an Assemblies of God church he attended on Baillou Road and Vesey Street. When the pastor made an altar call, I didn't care that I was the only one walking up that long, seemingly lonely aisle. I had had enough of the life I was living. I was about to crash and burn, and I had no one else to blame except myself. I realized that the choices I made in life were my choices, and they were bad. That day I gave my heart to the Lord Jesus Christ. I was determined to put the same effort and more into living for him as I did for the devil. I also committed to studying God's word, keeping company with those who would encourage me in my walk with Christ. I gradually shed my friends and my old habits. With each day, I became stronger. Not long after, it was clear how my lifestyle was impacting my family. My younger brother gave his life to the Lord and then my sister. Then Mom and, much later, my elder brother also came to know the Lord. Years later, after battling an illness, Dad followed suit. Though we didn't see him every day, we visited him through the years to let him know we loved him.

A Career Change

I had worked at Navios Shipping Corporation, which offered me a scholarship to be trained as a deck officer at Warsaw Maritime College in Southampton, England. The scholarship was withdrawn, and Navios moved its headquarters from New Providence to the U.S. It was a great disappointment. The Royal Bahamas Defence Force was established in March of that year. My mom later told me about the Bahamas government offering naval scholarships for young men to join. Within forty days, Cuban MiG jetfighters sunk HMBS Flamingo in May 1980. I applied to join the Force six months following the incident.

The Flamingo Incident occurred during the Cold War era, with escalating tensions between Russia, the United States, and their allies. I had a short interview with Commodore William Swinley, the first Commander Defence Force on loan from the Royal Navy. My application was accepted after being interviewed by the Officers Commission Board. I was among a group of ten persons selected and was part of the first five to be sent off to attend the Britannia Royal Naval College, a renowned naval training college in Dartmouth, England. The year of intense training at the college was the toughest I ever experienced. I wanted to quit during the very first term. But my faith in God and willingness to apply myself kept me in the game.

The second term was spent at sea learning the ropes, living the life as a deckhand and as a young naval officer under training while sailing to a number of European ports I had only dreamt of before. We circumnavigated Great Britain before sailing to Germany,

Denmark, Norway, and Sweden. The ship's company tracked Russian naval ships in the Baltic Sea, conducted missile test firings, and amphibious assaults ashore involving military tanks, helicopters, and the Royal Marines. After graduating, my course mates were called off to take part in the Falklands War. The ship I trained on, HMS Intrepid, was deployed to the frontlines.

While on my summer break following my sea training, I came across an evangelist who was having a crusade at Kensington Temple Church. He spoke a powerful faith message on not quitting and how we should at least make the first steps in the right direction and watch God move on our behalf as he did for the four lepers outside besieged Samaria's city gates. The message rose inside me and began driving me forward to acquire the Best International Midshipman Award.

Within a few weeks of completing my naval studies, I was in the heart of the action serving in the Royal Bahamas Defence Force. It was the peak of the drug trafficking era. I was appointed navigating officer of one of the most successful patrol craft in the Force, Inagua. Engaged in hot pursuits, firing warning shots at drug traffickers, intercepting major drug hauls, apprehending undocumented migrants, and capturing marine poachers were commonplace. It was during a time when the Bahamas was touted as a Nation for Sale. Several officials were implicated by the Commission of Inquiry into Narcotics Trafficking through the Bahamas Report (1983). I was involved in some of the largest drug busts in the Force's history during the drug era of the 80s. Knowing the life I had lived before, I was amazed at how God transformed my life.

I used my appointments and Christian witness to influence fellow Officers and hundreds of marines throughout my career in the Force. I spent much of my time helping others to get ahead, never realizing that one day I would become the Commander Defence Force. Though at times, my commitment to doing the right thing was not always accepted during the crucial era of the 80s, I was always willing to stand alone. At 21, I was appointed a commanding officer of a 60-foot patrol craft with a 14-man crew. But not everything was smooth sailing. Several years later, my gung-ho attitude caused me to throw caution to the wind. Instead of waiting out a passing storm that was moving through the northern Bahamas, I decided to make my way through a hazardous channel and ran aground amid a downpour of rain, strong winds, and high seas. Thankfully, no one was hurt, and the ship remained afloat. Apart from resistance from drug traffickers, this was the first harrowing experience. I lost three months' seniority. But without having time to sulk, Senior Commander Amos Rolle, the former commanding officer of HMBS Flamingo and then captain of Coral Harbour Base, assigned me to a larger vessel, immediately rebuilding my confidence. Twenty-two years later, I was appointed the commanding officer of HMBS Bahamas, a ship more than three times the size and over ten times the cost of the one I grounded.

Strengthening My Foundation

The Force had developed me to be accountable, manage responsibility, and live a disciplined life. I had also grown spiritually thanks to the profound teachings of Dr. Myles Munroe at Bahamas Faith Ministries. I was terrible with relationships due to the early training I received from my father, but I had enough sense to realize that I needed help in this area. In addition to reading his books and listening to his tapes, I had completed several of Dr. Munroe's extensive marriage preparation programs. His teaching resources had transformed me from a rambling hoodlum into a young man who respected and valued women.

Amazingly, the young lady who dumped me nine years before ended up attending Bahamas Faith Ministries. We got to talking, became friends, and in just over a year, we were married. It was one of the best decisions I ever made. I was an Assistant Staff Officer to the first Bahamian Commander Defence Force, Commodore Leon Smith when Teri and I were married. I had already served in the Force for about seven years. Three years later, I resigned from the Force. I thought I had experienced all the excitement a young man could have in a lifetime.

Commodore Smith was kind enough to accept my resignation in 1991, saying that he did not want me to leave the Force, but if I ever decided to return, he would be the first to let me back in. I left on a very high note, with no intentions of returning; I wanted to explore life on my terms. Thankfully, I did not voice what I was thinking. I ended up resigning from the Force for almost five years. During that period, my wife and I owned and operated a resort-wear manufacturing company, and I also conducted leadership training programs for young adults. A few years in, I also worked as the human resource manager at Trinity Air Bahamas. Throughout this period, I resisted an inner urge to return to the Force. I knew I was called to it. I also knew that if I went back, I would have lost five years of seniority and would have to start my career all over again.

Commodore (Ret.) Tellis A. Bethel Sr.

In wanting to pursue God's plan for my life rather than my own, I humbled myself, reapplied to join the Force, and was accepted. Sure enough, Commodore Smith was the first to welcome me back in 1996. Although I had lost seniority, I was happy to be where I believed God wanted me to be. I spent my time helping others succeed while bringing solutions to the table as a problem solver rather than a problem talker. I never knew fourteen years later, I would be appointed the Force's first Deputy Commander Defence

Force (2010-2015) and later appointed Commander Defence Force, spending five years in each post.

I didn't know that I would play a critical role in the modernization of the Force and overseeing some of the largest law enforcement operations, base development, ship and equipment acquisition, recruitment and youth (Rangers), and environmental conservation programs. This was done while laying a foundation for future Force personnel to build upon for generations to come.

More importantly, I never knew that Christ would have transformed my life from being a negative influencer to a positive influencer with responsibility for safeguarding an entire nation. The key, I have come to discover, is one's willingness to surrender to God to fulfill his call for one's life. One of the phrases Dad used was, "I can't lose for the stuff I use; I gotta win for the shape I'm in." Let me put that into perspective; you can't lose when you give your life to Christ and apply the principles of God's Word (the Bible) to every area of your life. It's at your point of surrender to him that you are empowered to truly live and fulfill your destiny.

Commodore (Ret.) Tellis A. Bethel Sr.

Commodore Tellis A. Bethel Sr., {retired} a former Commander Defence Force within the Royal Bahamas Defence Force (2015 – 2020), currently serves as the Standards Inspector of Security Forces within The Bahamas. As a naval officer, author, and historian, Commodore Bethel has been privileged to patrol the waters surrounding the 700 islands of The Bahamas. He has developed a distinct love for the historic waters of The Bahamas, and the story of the Lucayans, the extinct indigenous people of The Bahamas and Turks and Caicos Islands. Commodore Bethel is a lead proponent of naming the unnamed waters of the Bahamas the Lucayan Sea in memory of the native Lucayans.

A graduate of Saint John's College {Nassau}, the Britannia Naval College, Devon, England, and the Naval Staff College at the United States Naval War College in Providence, Rhode Island, Commodore Bethel has a Master of Arts degree in Leading Innovation and Change from York St. John University in England. He enjoys jogging, adventure travel, writing, and speaking on character and leadership development topics. He is married to Teri (née Knowles), and the couple has two adult sons.

Commodore Bethel's books are available in New Providence and Eleuthera and on Amazon.com in Kindle and paperback. He can also be reached at tbethel@tellisbethel.com.

SURVIVING DOMESTIC ABUSE

Dr. Deborah Pople-Smith

The phone rang, and the voice on the line asked if my newborn child had dropped its navel string. I thought it was a strange question, and after answering no, I thought her instructions were even more bizarre. Janet's instructions were for me to scrape the dry skin from beneath my feet and sprinkle it into the unhealed navel of my child. That way, she said, the child would never deny me anything. The concept did not sit right with me, so I didn't. However, I better understood why there seemed to be an insatiable desire to have things at her children's expense. Before taking care of their home and responsibilities, the matriarch came first. She had to have the best clothing, drive the latest car and be perfectly manicured from head to toe. If there was a shortfall, she reverted to the dark arts. In retrospect, I now understand why many children may be unable to say no to their parent's wishes even when it goes beyond their better judgment.

The Reality of The Spirit World

I understand that many people do not believe in the spirit world, but the truth is that it is more real than the physical world we live in. Just like I was at the time, people who do not have a personal relationship with Christ are affected by those who dabble in the dark arts to bring harm to them. At the time, I was overwhelmed; I didn't understand what I was seeing or why I was seeing it, yet what I saw was just as real as what I saw in the natural. Some may say that my mind was playing tricks on me. In fact, that was the plan. If Janet could make me and others believe that I had lost my mind, I would be out of the picture, and her plan for her son's life would continue. My sanity was undermined with her children, neighbors, and close friends. Her attempts were relentless in trying to have me fall under her pressure and agree that I had lost my mind. It was her word over mine. She and her family were highly regarded in the community. They were considered honorable and God-fearing people who were strong pillars of society, even though a visit to the sorceress was a regular occurrence for her.

As I looked through the corner of my eye, there appeared to be red lobsters the size of juvenile turtles crawling on the surface of my kitchen walls. They vanished into thin air when I turned to get a better look. This was a regular occurrence in my home at that time. There were days when I would see through the corner of my eye a headless man standing at the corner of my dining room table. He took on the form of a muscular bodybuilder with greased skin that started from his shoulders straight down. He was dark-skinned and had an arrowed-shaped tail. It was a frightening sight to see. Had I known the scripture in Isaiah 41:10 that encourages me not to fear, I would have been able to deal with the awful things I saw daily.

In the mornings, as I walked from my bedroom, down through the hallway to the kitchen, I would usually see a snake, approximately six-foot-long, wrapped up and relaxing on my beige sofa in my front room with its head poking out. On a good day, a precious beautiful little girl who looked to be not more than three or four years old, dressed in a gorgeous light pink dress with a pink bow in her afro hair, and soft pink ballerina slippers, danced near my bedroom door and in the hallway. Even though I would hear the noises she made, her face was blank, so there were no recognizable features visible.

The darkness that swept over Janet eventually made its way into my home, where infidelity and physical and emotional abuse became the norm. From the outside, we looked like the perfect family in a beautiful home with a well-manicured lawn and new vehicles parked in the driveway. From the inside, I was alone, hurting, abused, and broken, a woman desiring death more than believing it was possible to have a better life.

For many years, I asked God for his mercy. I wanted out of this situation. Sometimes I felt so alone; I thought I would die in this condition.

At night especially, I wondered if God heard me or if He would answer my prayer. I would listen to the words in the songs of Betty Jean Robinson, which provided temporary comfort; then, I would feel hopeless and become depressed. Though limp and tired, I took on the battle myself and was far from holding my peace. If I had the tears I shed in that period of my life, I believe I could have drowned in them. I was tired of fighting and thought death was the only way out of this horrific nightmare. At that time, I did not understand that God wanted me to let Him fight my battles. I now realize that I was not equipped with the word of God or divine strategies. I was no match for the enemy.

Feeling that I had come to the end of myself, with no hope for a brighter tomorrow, I took my little children to my sister in my moment of desperation. Unbeknownst to her, I said my goodbyes to them. I returned home and went into my master bedroom closet. I just wanted to end the pain and hurt that I was feeling. The noises in my head told me, "Girl, kill yourself! That will be good for him; he will be sorry for how he treated you!" These words sounded good because I was hurting so badly and looking for pity, not deliverance. I was looking for a way to get back at Janet and her son to make them pay. I wanted to make them sorry for what they were doing to me. The enemy's intention was for me to be out of the way. Janet intended to look like the loving and concerned in-law, and her offspring would take on the appearance of a loving and devoted husband who was unfortunate to have a wife with mental issues. Sadly, I was playing right into the enemy's hands.

Notwithstanding the mental gymnastics bouncing through my mind, I believed I had to commit suicide—there was no other way out of my situation. No one understood what I was feeling or how much pain I was experiencing. No one really cared. I thought I was all alone in the house, so I took off my wedding band and engagement ring, rested them on the top shelf in my closet, and prepared myself to exit this cruel world of agony and suffering.

Suddenly, I heard a still, calm, voice saying, "When you kill yourself, where will you spend eternity?" I was so afraid that I dropped everything and ran out of my closet. I searched the house, but there was no one there except me. This was all foreign to me because I was taught that the Holy Spirit existed, but I had no idea that he talked with us or played an essential part in our lives. Unfortunately, I was not taught or prepared for the storms of life or how to weather them.

Know Where You Are Getting Your Spiritual Food

The question God asked consisted of only nine words, but those nine words turned my life around. I cried out to the Lord to help me, and from that day onward, instead of watching the enemy, I began to pray more and study the scriptures. I didn't know until that point how important it was to be a part of a Bible-believing church. Unfortunately, many persons who are going through their storms believe that when they give their lives to Christ, the storms of life will cease. On the contrary! The enemy is angry because he lost a soul, so he intensifies the troubles in our lives to discourage us, hoping to get us back in his territory.

Being the merciful God, he reached out to me at my lowest, darkest moment despite not having a personal relationship with Christ even though I prayed and went to church. I was never taught that a personal relationship with Christ was important or how to achieve it. I needed to read the word of God daily and rely on the promises of God in the scriptures to sustain me. The enemy knew my plight, so he turned up the heat on me. After realizing a change in my life, Janet came after me with a vengeance. But God began to open my eyes to the enemy's plans. He told me things as I slept.

One night in a dream, I saw Janet. She came through my back door, followed by two men dressed in silver scissors tailcoat suits, and black top hats. These men seemed to be in a stupor because their eyes were focused only on her and never blinked. They kept their heads straight even when they stood at attention near her side. However, Janet never took her eyes off me; she carried a large brown paper bag as she moved toward the sitting room. While sitting in a white chair in the middle of that room, she began digging in her brown bag. Shortly after her digging began, my teeth seemed as if they turned into chalk and began to crumble. I could feel things moving around in my mouth, so I ran to the restroom to spit it out. When I got to the face basin, I heard a still, calm voice saying, "If you spit that out of your mouth, I will not have anything to purify." I awoke, trying to figure out what that dream meant. I knew Janet was working overtime trying to bring her spoken words to pass, and her offspring had no choice but to do whatever she told him. One evening, I overheard a telephone conversation with her son responding; he said, "No, she is not burning any candles, but she is always praying and using the olive oil."

The Guilt of Adulterous Affairs

Even though I suspected what was happening in my home, I was faithful to my vows and duties as a wife. The house was always cleaned, food cooked, bread or cakes baked, clothes washed, dried, and ironed. There was nothing in that area to use for starting an argument. Nevertheless, many mornings around 2:00 a.m., I was awakened for one silly reason or the other. So it was, as I was abruptly awoken from a deep sleep to hear the words, "Who that was you had in my car today?" Followed by a slap so hard that I saw lights, and it sent me flying out of my warm bed onto the hallway floor. When I finally caught myself, my face swelled until it was huge and black and blue. The pain was almost unbearable,

21

and I could not go to work for days with the disfigurement. In all the mental and physical abuse I had taken in the past, I knew I could no longer live under these circumstances. This behavior was unwarranted because there was no one in the car that day; it was his guilty conscience acting out.

The marriage only lasted a short time after that incident because he allowed the devil to fool him into coming after me again. I am not proud to say this, but this time, I snapped! I never knew that I could have so much rage in me. I don't remember the full details, but I was told that one of the little children called my older sister, and one child called the police. They were on speed dial for emergency purposes. When I came to my senses, there were four police officers dressed in brown, I dripped from head to toe in olive oil and had a 235-pound man dangling in mid-air. At that time, I was only 175 pounds. The bar was destroyed, and the front and living rooms were damaged. The police officers said they were tired of coming to the house to rescue me, so they took him away so that I would have time to make other permanent arrangements for the children and me. Shortly after that incident, I moved in with my sister until I could get a place for us.

God Is the Only Righteous Judge

My marriage ended in a bitter divorce—the thing I hated and had judged so many on. During my divorce, I learned how to lean and depend on Jesus; he was my lawyer and judge in the courtroom. Amid my turmoil, I learned how to turn my plate down, fast, and pray. I developed a good relationship with God. He became my husband, my friend, a father to my children, my deliverer, my Lord, and my Savior.

Don't Forget the Children

I had small children who loved and needed their father in their lives, but the enemy stole that from them. We sometimes forget the children when we go through life's storms while experiencing our pain and suffering. They may not be able to verbalize it depending on their age, but they also go through pain and suffering. These storms can affect them deeply. Thank God that I knew firsthand how these situations could traumatize children. Even though I got professional help for them early, they still live with the scars today.

Over the years, God has given me the strength to move on, and He has given me a testimony. Not only did God save me from eternal death and separation from him, but He also forgave all my sins, washed me in His precious blood, and filled me with His Holy Spirit.

He also gave me spiritual gifts that I never knew existed. God set me free from a life of uncertainty, pain, and torment.

After He delivered me, he prepared a wonderful man, just for me! Later, I decided to remarry, and God blessed our union with a beautiful addition to our family. Our marriage was not a bed of roses because the enemy would always raise his head in one way or the other. I sometimes reacted defensively to my husband, only to be told, "I am not him, but we will work this situation out together." God knew exactly who and what I needed to help me on life's journey and in this new season of my life. Marriage requires commitment and work, but if we want to be married, we must put God first and work on our relationships daily.

After a few years into my second marriage, the Holy Spirit spoke to me and told me to go to certain former family members and ask for their forgiveness. Well, I responded as most people would; I said, "Satan, I rebuke you in the name of Jesus!" Why do I have to go to them and ask for forgiveness? They were the ones who made my life a living hell and wished for my death. I didn't know at the time that forgiveness was just as much for me as it was for them. But God knew it and had a plan to safeguard my future. If I didn't walk in forgiveness, I couldn't expect the same from the Lord.

Many years have passed, and the persons responsible for bringing much misery and pain to my life have also experienced storms. As I thought about what God told me to do, these words came to me:

When in affliction's valley, I'm treading the road of care,

My Savior helps me to carry my cross when heavy to bear.

My feet entangled with briars, ready to cast me down.

My Savior whispered His promise, never to leave me alone.

No, never alone, No, never alone, He promised never to leave me,

Never To Leave Me Alone.

The Holy Spirit did not leave me alone. He repeated the words, "Go and ask so and so to forgive you." This was not an easy task, but I knew God's voice by then, so I asked for forgiveness. Shortly after I went to one of the individuals in question, they departed this life.

A Time for Forgiveness and Healing

I'm grateful to God for allowing me to truly forgive those who hurt me; I can finally put the past where it belongs, in the past! But I'm reminded of the scripture in Colossians 3 that says, "He that doeth wrong shall receive for the wrong which he hath done."

When their troubles began, I thought I would be happy and say, "That's good for them," but it was the opposite. I had compassion for them because I knew they would die and go to hell if they did not repent for their sins. The word of God says it is not God's will that any should perish but that all will repent of their sins. I prayed for them that God would have mercy on them and bring them to true repentance. Janet, who was determined to destroy me, has lost her spouse, some children, other family members, and finally, her health. The enemy always pays his faithful servants in sickness, crisis, disappointments, trouble, an unfulfilled life, and sometimes death for the service that they render to him. As for her son, he took terrible advice, lost his faithful wife, and missed out on the years of his precious children growing up in his home; those memories are lost from him forever.

A short time ago, I met Janet and her family. It was good seeing them all. The most profound thing about the visit was that there was no animosity in my heart, and they were thankful that I had accepted their invitation. God had truly done a work in me to forgive them, notwithstanding that 100% of my marital problems could not be attributed to my former husband and his family. I realize that I, too, could have done some things differently.

I was fortunate to be able to return to the classroom some years ago; today, I am an ordained minister with a master's degree in Christian counseling and a doctorate in ministry. I am very active in a Bible-believing church, where I spread the good news of salvation by teaching and preaching God's word.

The enemy wants to destroy your present life and the blessed hope of living and reigning with Christ. He wants to alter the plans of God for your life, to stop you from fulfilling your destiny. If you are a new convert and it seems since committing your life to Christ, things appear to go wrong, you should know that being a Christian does not stop the attacks from coming your way; instead, as a Christian, you can have insider knowledge through the Holy Spirit and the word of God to equip you to overcome the enemy, just as he did with me.

Dr. Deborah Pople-Smith

Deborah Pople-Smith, Ph.D., has served in various roles in her local church and is an ordained pastor, and Christian Counselor. Dr. Pople-Smith preaches and teaches the good news of the Kingdom of God through zoom services, Bible Study, and workshops. She obtained her Bachelor's degree in Ministry from Revelation Bible College, a Master's of Arts degree in Christian Counseling, and a Doctorate degree in Ministry from Jacksonville Theological Seminary, Jacksonville Florida. She is married to Baldwin Smith; the couple has six adult children and five grandchildren. Her hobbies are fishing, sewing, and crafting. The Smiths reside on the beautiful island of Freeport in Grand Bahama, The Bahamas.

Dr. Pople-Smith's book Unbroken Generational Curses, How to Be Set Free, can be found on Amazon.com in Kindle or paperback.

FREEDOM BEHIND BARS

Theo O. Rolle

Stacked in neat rows of three like sardines in a heat-sealed can dripping with stale sweat, and closer than most people want to be with anyone, inmates of Her Majesty's Fox Hill Prison lay lengthwise on the cold, bare cement floor of our unlit cell. To our heads sat one on the bucket that served as the toilet for five grown men in a cell that had yet to be cleaned in all my years as a resident of the facility. The bucket he sat on would be emptied in the morning. His head and back pressed to the wall in one position, hoping for some shuteye before morning and relief from the obnoxious odor that seeped through not just our bucket but all the buckets on our windowless maximum security block. Across our feet in front of the steel doors lay another inmate. Even as a man of average height, he was too tall to stretch out completely in the tiny cell that should house one or maybe two people at best. He was our buffer, the one who served as the first trampoline for the hungry resident rodents and roaches that climbed our makeshift cardboard barricade at the base of the iron gate for the little food we stashed in plastic bags tied to the bars. We were L7, one of the twelve cells on the block who endured a harsh life in prison.

My Early Life

Nobody plans to fall flat on their face. And I don't know of anyone who planned to spend time in prison. I didn't, but that's where I ended up early in life. Not once, or twice, not even three times. No, I found myself in the literal hell hole, eight, maybe nine times because of my poor decisions. Stay with me as I share my journey and how I experienced freedom behind bars.

Theo Rolle being held by his mother as a baby.

As a young boy growing up in a fatherless home with my mother and four siblings, I realized early that I didn't just want a daddy; I needed one. Boys in particular, love comradery. They are born to lead but need to be taught how to. In the absence of having a father or a positive male role model in our lives, we seek the next best thing, a counterfeit of the original. Some boys in my day, and now even girls, look to have this need met by becoming a part of a gang. By virtue of living in a particular neighborhood, you were considered a gang in that specific area. I never saw myself as a gang member. I didn't see any benefit to it, and I wanted to live life on my terms, even as a kid. Life wasn't easy growing up, but Mummy did the best she could with me and my brother and our three sisters. I don't know if she realized it, but she was way out of her depth. She tried to be a mother and father but that was impossible. Mummy worked hard and was able to feed our bodies as best she could with the limited finances she had, but she couldn't feed the longing in my soul for my father.

Theo O. Rolle (Age 11)

Raised By a Single Mother

My mother probably got irritated with me asking the same questions day in and day out. Who is my daddy? Where is my daddy? Why isn't my daddy around? Of all my siblings' fathers, only one of them ever contributed to their child's well-being. Nevertheless, despite the heartbreak, I don't believe I was a troublesome child—I was confused and felt abandoned by the one person I believe a boy needed, his father. Without a father to help form my identity and guide me, I didn't know who I was or where I was going in life. Without knowing where I was going in life, I took the road of least resistance, a road my mother never approved of, the road that kept me in a cycle that took me nowhere.

Mummy laid down the law in our home. Sadly, it was not enough to keep me reined in. By the age of eleven, I believed I was my own man, and I was already spending much of my time on the streets. Mummy didn't like it, but I was prepared to suffer the consequences of my actions, even if it meant a good cut behind.

In my eyes, she was a woman, and no matter how hard she beat me, I would get over the pain quickly and do what I wanted to. I didn't believe a woman could relate to a male child as effectively as a man, no matter how well-intended she was.

Whenever she tried to discipline me, I retaliated by staying out later, knowing she would be worried. In my mind, if I was going to suffer, she would have to feel that too. So, I continued to spend time on the streets, connecting with the wrong fellas and eventually peddling drugs to help pay the bills around the home.

Even with spending most of my free time on the street, I was a good student. I remember being excited about going to school, I wanted an education, and I loved to learn. That was until the bullies decided I would be the object of their torment. They were groups of boys who were a part of a gang that was at war with the gang in my neighborhood. They didn't understand, nor did they care that I was not a part of the gangs in my neighborhood. By virtue of my address, I was not one of their crew—that made me bait, and they were the fish. If it were one or two boys, I would have been inclined to fight back, but I was outnumbered. I decided to keep calm and not make the situation any worse. Day after day, I ran home, trying to avoid the boys who were hell-bent on making my life miserable. At first, they surrounded me, taunting me with brutal words, they stole my lunch money, and on one occasion after buying lunch, one of them emptied it onto the ground. I was their target for rock-throwing when trying to go to a class.

At 14, I made up my mind that I would run no more—instead, I would put an end to my torment. That day, I packed a short cutlass in my school bag. I knew my tormentors could not resist having another go at me, and when they came, I was ready. After wielding the cutlass unmercifully, the well-slashed boys were carted off to the hospital, and me, to jail. Thankfully I got off that time, but it came with a heavy price: I was expelled from school with no hope of acceptance to any other school. With very little education, I joined the workforce pumping gas at a local service station. While working at the station, I heard about a program called YEAST. I was intrigued and wanted to be a part of it, so I spoke with several people who helped to get me into the program—although much of the focus was on math and English, being mentored by a man intrigued me. When I was nineteen, my mother died. It was a blow knowing that the one person who believed that I could do better was now gone.

A Life of Crime

As I grew, I didn't have the education or skills to equip me for an honest, well-paying job. The only thing I knew and was good at that could pay my bills was selling drugs. It didn't take long for me to become one of the better salesmen in a local drug ring. I worked hard, was paid well, and kept my mouth shut, sometimes being the fall guy for the bigger bosses without having to be asked. This lifestyle is what initially landed me behind bars at sixteen in 2004. Too many people on the outside believe breaking the law is cool and crime pays well. Thanks to Hollywood, those same people are duped into thinking a life of crime is glamorous and that spending

31

time in prison with their boys is not a bad deal.

You would think that one night in a hot crowded cell with food not fit for humans would be a deterrence to any misguided soul, but that is not the case. Instead, young men like me pour into the prison system like sheep being led to the slaughter daily. Some are falsely accused, others guilty of their crime.

Whether guilty or innocent, if you weren't in maximum security, you were afforded 20 minutes of free time outside your cell each day. You could use your time to shower in an open room with other inmates, or you had 20 minutes in the yard to exercise or meet up with friends from another block.

When it was time to eat, we had room service courtesy of the inmates' kitchen, cooked by inmates, and transported in the filthiest rat-infested old bus on the property. The food was served from large pots resting on rusty carts that looked and sounded like they would not make it to the end of the block by inmates who were not imprisoned for being kind or friendly. Most of us knew that if there was a hit placed on our heads, eating food that could be tampered with was the easiest way to satisfy a grudge. Those who did not have someone bringing them food had to eat the unsightly, lousy-tasting food or at the least trade money, cigarettes, or drugs with other inmates who had food delivered. I could not, would not eat the food that I had on occasion watched being prepared by grown men with their sweat dripping from their dirty, greasy skin into the pots. I ate peanut butter sandwiches and, for breakfast corn flakes when I had them in my personal stash. If I was fortunate, I could trade a joint for KFC or a similar fast-food from the inmates in remand. Remand inmates had more privileges and often had family and friends bringing them food daily.

Charged With Murder

I was at my lowest point after being charged with murder and sentenced to 58 years in prison. Unfortunately, I was in the wrong place at the wrong time with a firearm. I enjoyed going to nightclubs and was at one with a girl when we heard gunshots. In the confusion of people screaming and running I saw a gunman running towards us. Instinctively I pulled out my weapon and unloaded it on him. In my mind, it was shoot or be shot. Regrettably, the man died, I was arrested and lost my case—it was back to the Fox Hill hellhole I had come to hate. My punishment was more severe. There were days I did not see the light of day. My morale began to wane, and my body was becoming deficient in nutrients causing severe hair loss. There was nothing to do there unless you were considered low to medium security risk and then you may be fortunate to work. With countless hours on my hand, I found myself talking to God and reading my Bible.

To my surprise, the Father began talking to me—his voice was crystal clear. I found out that despite being in prison, he was with me and had not forgotten about me. He wanted to be the father I never had. It was then I wanted nothing else but to live. He said he would give me another chance of freedom—he wanted me to live for him. One night as I slept, I was taken up to Heaven. It was a spiritual encounter. My physical body remained in the cell but I was totally aware of where I was and who I was with. I saw the streets of gold; I saw angels and people singing and rejoicing. When I woke up, I told my cellmates about the encounter, but they did not believe me. At that point, people's opinions of me didn't matter anymore. I promised God that I would not wait until he got me out of prison to live for him, and I would live for him from that moment on. I felt free, even though I was caged like an animal behind bars. Of course, my fellow inmates were taken aback at first. They were amused and openly ridiculed me, but I knew that God was speaking to me, and his opinion of me was more important than what they or anyone else thought of me.

A Change Has to Come

I was full of joy and had great hope for better days ahead. I knew I had to do something about the love of God that continued to build within me. I wanted to sing, to praise God, and give him thanks for who he was and what he had kept me from. I believed with all my heart that God would have me vindicated, but I couldn't in all good conscience wait until then to thank him for his goodness. One day I announced to the entire block that we would begin singing praises to God every morning. I loved to sing and could manage to hold a melody. We started with some of the old familiar songs I remembered from when I went to church with my mother as a boy.

The first man to join me was a rough Rasta who nobody dared to talk to about God. He was fierce. But God touched him, and it triggered a ripple effect throughout the block where even the most God-resistant men began singing praises to God. Sometime later, I made another announcement, that we would do the same in the evening. We did and it was wonderful. Little by little you could see a softening of some of the men's hearts to God. Soon eight years had passed, and my case was up for retrial. Many naysayers were happy to tell me that I would never win the case and would remain in prison. The God I served had other plans and made them plain for everyone to see.

With the testimony of a witness, I won the case and was released from prison in 2016. I believe God used my life as a testimony to show my fellow inmates how good he really is. It built their faith and kept them singing long after I had been released. Some of the brothers gave their lives to the Lord, which encouraged me to return several times to visit, hoping to strengthen their faith, but I was eventually asked by an employee of the prison not to return. They said that I had served my time and did not need to come back. When inmates were released, however, I knew they needed a support system on the outside and was there to encourage them to walk uprightly and live for God.

Living On the Outside

My time on the outside was not without its challenges. I had grand plans to succeed with my newfound freedom. Unfortunately, my finances began to dwindle before any of my plans materialized. After having exhausted all my money, I had to move out of the place I lived. I was homeless. I had nothing and nowhere to go. It seemed like my dreams had dried up with my money. At the time,

I was too proud to ask for help and ended up sleeping on park benches at night until I reached out to a local ministry that took in men.

That went well for a while, and I was grateful for a roof over my head and food to eat. In spite of my gratitude for the place opening its doors to me, I became aware of a troubling pattern in the home and brought it to the attention of the director, who was not happy with my observations or my willingness to let them know what I thought about the matter. I was told I had to leave immediately. I requested one more night, which was graciously allowed. That night I prayed like never before and decided to bury my pride. I called my friends and family and for the first time, was completely candid with them about what I was going through. The overwhelming love and support that was showered on me landed me in my own apartment with all my needs being met.

I was given the opportunity to work at a hotel on Paradise Island for a while in the banquet department, only to have to leave after the lockdown. Not being one to wait for opportunities to knock on my door, I began a mobile car wash service where I took my business to my clients. During this time, I connected with a local church that has been a tremendous support to me. In addition to working with them, I've had the opportunity to spearhead three feeding programs in the neighborhood where we take food to the hungry and share the word of God with them.

My greatest joy is to go from door to door every weekend, to share the goodness of God and plates of food with my community. I'm amazed how this kind gesture provides an opportunity for people who are many times as lost and broken as I was. They are grateful to have a conversation with someone who is willing to listen to them and satisfy the hunger in their bellies and hearts. In my quiet moments, I wonder how many young boys are like I was, looking for their fathers or someone to father or mentor them. How many are like me who chose the streets or gangs because they aren't aware of an alternative? Some single mothers raise their children well, but boys need a real father in their lives. A man who would affirm and encourage him. A man who would teach him right from wrong and be prepared to live by example.

I give God praise for where he has brought me in my relationship with him. But could it have been different? Could it have been better for me and many young men who wasted years living fruitless lives, if we had a strong family unit with a father who invested time, love, and resources into our lives?

Theo O. Rolle at work

Not every home with a father and a mother turns out well, but history has shown over the years that children with a responsible father in their lives stand a better chance of succeeding in life and avoiding prison. With studies in the United States revealing that the majority of black inmates were raised by single mothers, it gives us reason to pause and think about our decisions in having children and raising them according to God's plan.

Theo O. Rolle

Theo O. Rolle is a resilient man with a colored past and a bright future. Mr. Rolle loves to share his story with others with the hope of encouraging them to ensure that they get their lives in order. During his free time, he likes to organize feeding opportunities for the underprivileged in the various communities. Mr. Rolle is actively involved in his local church.

He currently works for a Bahamian company that creates and installs awnings and canopies for boats and buildings throughout the Bahamas. Mr. Rolle considers himself blessed that the company's owner reached out to him at a critical time in his life and mentored him with a skill. He is a native Bahamian and the father of two beautiful children.

OVERCOMING THE EMOTIONAL PAIN OF INCEST

Brenda Dewis

The missing pieces of my shattered life came together when I was twenty-six. I was at a function and met a young man and decided I would go with him to the movies. We hit it off quite well, and the evening looked promising until my aunt told us that we had to cancel the outing. The reason, she claimed, was that the young man was my father's son, my brother. The news took me for a loop. "My brother?" I knew I had two younger brothers, but the young man standing before me was not one of them. She explained that his father was my father and the man I grew up thinking was my father was not. I was confused but somewhat relieved.

You see, the man I had grown up calling Daddy was the father to my two younger brothers. The story was more convoluted than I wanted to know at the time. My biological father was related to the family who brought my mother from Haiti. He took advantage of her, and she became pregnant with me. Mummy never spoke of it, and even when I asked her, being a woman of very few words, she merely said that my aunt talked too much.

Then Who Is My Daddy?

Well, things began to make a little more sense to me. So, the man I called Daddy was not my father. Was that why he could sexually abuse me for so long?

A part of me was relieved that we were not related, but how could a grown man be so cold-hearted in taking advantage of an innocent child?

I did some backtracking in my mind. I didn't have to think too deeply. I was washing the dishes one evening when the man I had come to know as Daddy approached me and told me that since my mother was not giving "it" to him, I would have to. I was twelve years old, tall and developing physically, but not wise to sex as my mother had not spoken to me about the facts of life. If I wasn't sure what he was saying then, I found out later that night after he had his usual round of drinks.

Before this transpired, I thought I lived a normal life as a child. We weren't wealthy, but my parents ensured my siblings and I were well cared for. The first home I recall living in was off Wulff Road. When I was seven years old, we moved to a southern subdivision. Mummy was a hardworking lady who often held down two jobs, and on occasion, her day job extended into the night as she was a housekeeper and a cook. There were times Mummy traveled with the families she worked for, which sometimes meant I had to sleep at my aunt's house—I didn't understand why at the time, but as my thoughts settled, the pieces of my life came together. Mummy's life was not easy, but she was not a complainer; she was a soft-spoken but firm individual who laid down the law with her children.

It wasn't until I was older that I learned a little about my mother's past. She was born and raised in Haiti at a time when Haiti was the place where Bahamians in the southern Bahamas frequented for shopping, visits to the doctor, and, like many in the region, holidays. She was from Port de Paix, a more developed part of the country. For some, it was more economical to travel to Haiti than to the capital city of Nassau. Haiti was a bustling country that was more advanced in many ways than many of the outer islands of the Bahamas.

On such a visit, a family who frequented Haiti on business spoke with my mother's family, offering to bring her to the Bahamas to enroll in school, despite Haiti's vast educational system at the time. They promised that they would ensure her return to them on holidays. It was an opportunity the family embraced. Mummy said her goodbyes and made her way to Nassau. As promised, she was enrolled in school. However, for some reason unknown to me, she was never allowed to return to Haiti. That's when the man I grew up calling Uncle forced himself on Mummy when she was nineteen, and I was born. I don't know if how I was conceived affected our relationship, but I realized early that it was strained. There were no arguments, just little communication. Despite this, I knew Mummy loved me, and her way of communicating was to provide for me.

My Unwelcomed Visitor

The night Daddy said he was coming to my room, he remained true to his word. His plan, however, was foiled by Mummy. I had confided in her what he had said earlier, so when she checked on me that night, her husband was fumbling by my bedside with the excuse that he was checking on me—just fixing my bed. She calmly asked him not to, and the next day, Mummy bought me a night latch for my bedroom door. The night latch was a small challenge for Daddy. He was a carpenter by trade, and even though I had latched the door, he was able to make his way into the room—possibly with the knife he often carried as he approached my bed. Once inside, he would relatch it, so Mummy thought I was asleep. Daddy told me I was helping Mummy out since she wasn't having sex with him, but he wanted it to be our secret. She would have been angry if she had found out, but he claimed it was for her good.

For the next two years, Daddy sneaked into my bedroom, latched the door behind himself, and told me to lay on the floor. I didn't like what he was doing to me; I didn't want him to touch me the way he did night after night. I was confused, and it was painful just as he said it would be, yet he continued despite the obvious pain and trauma it was causing. Sometimes he stayed through the night, wanting to repeat his assault on my young, tired, and now sore body. I couldn't understand why my father would do such a thing, but I began to think it was normal because I was not told otherwise. I began to think all girls had to go through this. I started to hate being a girl—I wanted to be a boy so that no one would abuse me. I didn't realize it at the time, but that was a plan of the enemy to push me towards same-sex attraction. The violation had opened the door for me to entertain the thought, and after a superficial encounter, it didn't feel right. I realized it was not the thing to do.

During the day, he was a normal father, although he was aggressive with Mummy, which often ended with her being physically beaten. We had family nights on Fridays and went to the drive-in theater, and on Saturdays, we went out for treats.

No one would have suspected that he was a beast at night with the child who called him Daddy. I was fearful, but fear had become my norm—I had nobody to speak to about what was happening to me.

I wondered if I didn't do what he said, if he would beat me the way he beat my mother. I didn't want to find out, so I did not resist or speak to my mother on the subject again. A part of me, though, believed that she knew what was going on.

How Or Why Did It Stop?

The sexual abuse triggered anger, making me want to lash out at men. Then I became promiscuous. Not to enjoy sexual encounters;

in my young mind, I thought I was paying the young men back for what had happened to me. I wanted them to feel the pain inflicted upon me by another man. It didn't take long to discover that my plan was not working. The only one being hurt in the charade was me. I had allowed myself to become bitter, and it was affecting me more than anyone else. To this point, my mother had never spoken to me about birth control or my period until I told her that I thought I had missed my period. I knew that when my father molested me, he wore condoms, but that was not the case during my years of promiscuity. After confiding in my mother that I believed that I had missed my period, she whisked me off to the doctor for birth control. The doctor inserted a coil, but that failed, leaving me pregnant at 19. I knew I had to get my life together. I felt like I was crumbling from the inside out.

Even with the trauma at home, we were a church-going family. We knew of God but did not know God; we went through the motions without having a functional relationship with Jesus Christ. It was becoming more evident that our religion did nothing to soothe the pain and confusion I was experiencing. I was invited to a church that was more Bible-based in its teaching. I felt there might be hope for me for the first time in my life. One day I listened to a teaching by a visiting pastor. What she said resonated with me, and I confided in her about what had happened in my youth. She listened intently. I didn't feel as though she was judging me. She was kind and compassionate but firm. I had to make up my mind to forgive my stepfather, or the hurt would continue. I was allowing the pain to root and flourish by not forgiving him. I wondered why it felt as though this ominous, dark, weighty cloud followed me for years like a pet on a leash. I wanted to be done with it; I had to, as she said, cut it free, deny its right to have access to me.

The minister told me to write my father's name on the paper and place it in an empty paper bag. She instructed me to take the bag and bury it. It was a symbolic representation of a spiritual gesture of cutting myself free of my past and burying all the pain and fear. I eagerly did as she said, desperately wanting to be free. I didn't care anymore who knew. If exposing the source was going to bring healing, then I had to do it or continue dying on the inside as I lived on the path of destruction. She led me in a prayer of forgiveness and repentance, and I immediately felt a massive weight lift from my shoulders. I felt new; I felt peace and joy.

For the first time in a long while, I believed I could live my life without being drenched in shame. I realized then that unforgiveness could no longer be a part of my life. Not just with my stepfather or my mother: I couldn't give the enemy a foothold in any area of my life if I were to remain free. I had the opportunity to confront my stepfather years later, but he had no remorse. He suggested I get over it as it happened long ago. His response saddened me, but I knew at least I had given him an opportunity to apologize and even repent for what he had done. Unfortunately, my mother and I never spoke of what had happened all those years ago, but our relationship never advanced to a pleasant one. One of my greatest regrets in life, however, was not going to see my biological father when he called for me before he passed away.

Helping Those Who Were Hurt

My desire is to now help others who have experienced the same brutality I did. It may not have been with a family member; it may have been a friend or a stranger. It doesn't matter, the violation is real and does not minimize the pain felt. In speaking with ladies devastated by incest or sexual abuse, they often claim they cannot share their stories for fear of reprisal in their families. This often compounds the shame and the pain the victim is going through. Like myself, many females and males who have been sexually violated have thought about and, in many cases, pursued same-sex relationships. Sadly, this is a trap of the enemy.

A website called winteryknight.com posted an interesting article several years ago that I thought was very informative. The article *Domestic Violence Rates Are Higher For Homosexual Couples Than For Heterosexual Couples*, provides statistics the younger me would have liked to have had back in the day. You see when the opposite sex hurts you, you are sometimes inclined to believe that partnering with your sex is a safer alternative. However, the studies in this article and others show that domestic violence in some cases, are at the same level as a heterosexual (man and woman) couple and some reports show that the abuse is even higher with homosexual or same-sex couples.

You want to experience love, and you deserve it, that is how God made you—to be a giver and a receiver of love. You may not feel you can trust the opposite sex after a violation, or you have a deep fear of them. My friend, don't let the enemy trick you into believing that is the way to go. It's a door that can be easily walked into but very difficult to walk out of. There are bad people in this world, both men and women. However, just because they are awful people doesn't make all men and all women bad. I'm happy I decided that I would maintain a relationship with the opposite sex as God designed. Despite my troubled past, he gave me a wonderful husband who not only knew my past but has loved me and treated me with respect for the past 30 years of our marriage. It takes courage to do the right thing. Bad things happen to good people, but you can make the right decision and invite God into your situation. Not religion, as I had initially, but a relationship with Jesus Christ who can lift your burden and break every chain in your life. I was tormented, but he gave me peace—I believe he would do the same for you if you asked.

I encourage those who have suffered this way to seek help. Pain does not stay buried. Perhaps in sharing your story responsibly, you will be helping others as my story has helped many. And it may be that the person who has hurt you would be compelled not to hurt anyone else. Whatever you decide, know that you can be free. I could have been free sooner, but I'm glad I found someone who knew God's word and could lead me from the dark world I was living in. Perhaps today will be your day for the same.

Brenda Dewis

Mrs. Dewis shares her testimony with both the young and older women on an individual basis, with the hope of them experiencing freedom from their pain and shame. She resides with her husband and their children in the Bahamas.

THE ROAD TO EMANCIPATION

Dr. Deborah Bartlett

Living a public life as a private person has its own set of challenges, especially when you sit where I sat for many years. My career began some years ago as a news reporter in the Bahamas. I became a news anchor and television program host for "Reaction" and "Woman," hosting big and small names both nationally and internationally at ZNS TV for 20 years. As a young reporter, my job took me in front of country heads such as Sir Lynden Pindling, the first prime minister of the Bahamas, and subsequent prime ministers in the person of the Rt. Hon. Hubert Alexander Ingraham, and the Rt. Hon. Perry Gladstone Christie. I also interviewed the former president of South Africa, the late Nelson Mandela, and the chairman of Heinz, Dr. Tony O'Reilly. It would be easy to become prideful at this point, but even if I leaned towards that road, I had parents, especially a mother, the late Mizpah Bartlett, who would yank me back in line, and my father Frank Bartlett, also deceased, whose quiet but firm strength played a role in keeping me grounded. No, it was a case of my gift

47

making room for me. It was also a case of putting into practice the art of finding solutions to problems. That may sound glamorous, but it wasn't. In fact, many days I wanted to throw in the towel, especially when things got challenging and uncomfortable. Nevertheless, as a journalist with a B.A. in Communications, I showed up at my job prepared to work.

L-R: Dr. Deborah Bartlett with the late Nelson Mandela, former President of South Africa.

People who saw me day in and day out on television think they know you. They believe that what they see is the total of who you are. They didn't know the preparation and investment, the long days and sleepless nights. They didn't see the island hopping on small planes and encountering dangerous weather as we flew the length and breadth of the country. What they knew and appreciated was my professional persona as a journalist. I was grateful for that.

In my early days, I worked hard, and yes, I partied just as hard. Partying drew many friends and acquaintances, but I realized that instead of empowering me, these associations were draining my creativity, strength, and ability to pursue the innate gifting that had to be nurtured by people who had my back and had achieved so much more than I had. Some would call it wisdom; others sobriety; I called it destiny. I came to faith in Christ, which set me on an even more intense trajectory.

> *It wasn't just a journey of skill and accomplishments I was on; now, it was one of character development at an even higher level in my pursuit of purpose.*

In striving for higher heights, I began to soar professionally. However, the higher I climbed, I found the altitude pruning relationships that were not headed in the same direction. It also caused discomfort with others who could not handle the incremental success even though it made them look good. Such was the case with one of my superiors, a senior manager. No matter what I did, it was not good enough. The verbal assaults launched at me so fiercely that I decided to approach the individual, apologizing for whatever I had done to offend her. I wanted to make it right. Initially, it caused some discomfort, but I kept going; if I were to succeed in life, I knew it wouldn't be because of popularity but my commitment to hard work. My good intention was met with fierce anger as I was booted from the office.

Nevertheless, I continued to do my job to the best of my ability. Sometime later, the senior manager became ill. Though she had not been kind to me, I was heartbroken to know she was suffering; I prayed for her. Before she died, she called for me, asking me to come and visit her. As soon as I walked into the room she told me that I had done nothing wrong, she apologized for her attitude towards me and asked me to forgive her. It was important for her to make things right with me before she met her maker. Before I left, she asked me to pray for her, and I did. I was never one to hold a grudge toward anyone or burn bridges. Had I hardened my heart towards her or burned the bridge of communication, it would have made it difficult to have the conversation we had. It was a lesson I learned early, and one I still practice today along with keeping a tight lip. That way those who hang around for morsels to repeat will not be able to misrepresent what you say. I knew I had already forgiven her and accepted her apology so there was no discomfort to deal with.

Deborah Bartlett, Reporter/Talk Show Host

I learned in life that offenses affect the offended more than the offender, so I made it my business not to allow anything or anyone to wear me down or hamper my relationship with the Lord. That mindset took me through many a difficult journey as I stepped out into the business and investments arena. My company, the CEO Network, was designed to help strengthen the work ethic, raise levels of productivity, and serve as a networking platform for economic empowerment. The motto of the CEO Network is "Empowering Professionals through Knowledge and Opportunities." This was just one of the endeavors my mother helped formulate alongside me. Among my business pursuits was pioneering a local radio station GEMS News Media Network, which had strategic relationships with some of the biggest media empires in the United States and the Caribbean.

L-R: HRH Princess Moradeun Ogunlana, Dr. Deborah Bartlett & HRH Princess Moradeun Adedoyin-Solarin (Nigeria)

While I was blessed with a good number of committed professionals, there were wolves in sheep's clothing at every turn, and unfortunately, some sheep who didn't know their identities trying to dress up as wolves. When you thought you swung around the bend to avoid them, in swam the sharks with sharpened teeth, looking to devour everything I had worked so hard for. Some skillfully infiltrated the ranks; others fell short. There was a siphoning of funds, equipment, and manpower in the process, coupled with death threats and near hits as I faced gunmen seeking to end my life.

At this time, the covering by local and foreign spiritual giants stood by me, deflecting attacks before they had a chance to land. It was also a time when the mentoring by business greats increased, which helped keep me focused. We had partnered on numerous business projects, and their wisdom was heartening. Friends and colleagues such as Richard Demeritte, former auditor general of the Bahamas, international singer and songwriter Candy Staton, Joe L. Dudley, Sr., co-founder and the mastermind behind the creation of the Dudley Q+brand, and the Dudley's Beauty University, and syndicated talk show host Armstrong Williams, remained fortresses in my business life.

Despite the challenges, I remained resolute in my faith. The same God who made me and blessed me would, in my opinion, restore me. The millions of dollars in contracts and the lives of my faithful employees now destitute of a job were above my pay grade—it was something I had to give Heaven to watch over. Like in my early days, the pruning of friends began. This time it wasn't because I was soaring; I was plummeting faster than I had climbed. It was a lonely season, seeing some of the very people you gave your last to, fought for, encouraged, trained, and celebrated turn on you like a flip of a switch. The propaganda swirled, but few thought to verify the information. They swallowed the lies in one gulp. That too, was shocking.

It amazed me that people who knew you for years never factored in your character or track record. I knew it was yet another thing I had to put into God's hands. Vindication had to come.

It didn't come as quickly as I wanted it to, but slowly, some returned to apologize, just as my former senior colleague had done. They realized they had been sold a lie and were ashamed they had bought it. Some admitted to influencing others to publicly slant stories to aid in my demise, stories they were told that were contrary to what they knew of me. The damage had been done, but the lessons for me were learned. I had to learn who to trust, how much to trust, and who to never trust. Former friends had aligned themselves with the enemy's camp.

The enemy I'm referring to is not an individual. Demonic entities use individuals to wreak havoc in the earth realm against the plans of God and his people. Instead of fighting against the thing that is empowering and causing people to do evil, we fight the people. That's like hosing down the smoke and not touching the fire. My company was pursuing God's agenda on a national and international level. It was easy for the enemy to find a group of people willing to put their plan before God's own. To take what God created to try to manipulate systems for their gain. Just like a spoilt child who cannot have his way in a game of marbles, the dust is kicked, marbles picked up, and the game is over.

If you are not careful, you can become caught up with the temper tantrums of the enemy rather than focusing on your mission. My company's vision is beyond me, beyond our borders; it's a global initiative to cause the economic emancipation of a people. Visions won't die if they're from God. A vision is a living organism that cannot die. However, it can be diverted. Although Gems was and still is celebrated by many in the country who benefited from the tremendous services offered, there were those who fought the notion of economic emancipation. The vision tarried, but it did not falter as it has now been embraced by several African nations.

So how did we get here as a people? Can we learn to advance together, or will we allow a few naysayers to stench against us as we press towards national advancement? As a Christian nation, our behavior has not been aligned with our talk. We've had so many people in our nation stain our soil with their sweat as they fought for equality and opportunity, such as the late Sir Randol Fawkes. We've had ambassadors in the sports and acting fields like the late Andre Rogers, a baseball Hall of Famer, a successful Hollywood actor, the late Sir Sidney Poitier, and many others who still do their part in putting our nation on the map. We've had the privilege of being led by spiritual generals and pioneers like the late Dr. Susan J. Wallace and Dr. Myles Munroe.

These were people of vision, who had a dream and set standards in their callings. In speaking for my long-time friend Dr. Bernice King at the service for her late father, Dr. Martin Luther King Jr., one of my childhood heroes at the annual ecumenical service in

2018, I told the viewers that destiny has predetermined that a Bahamian woman of color would be invited to the United States of America to speak on such a historic occasion.

L-R: The late Dr. Myles Munroe & Dr. Deborah Bartlett

I was deeply humbled and did not take the opportunity lightly. It was an opportunity for me to make Bahamians and the people of our region proud like so many before me had done. It's not until we learn to stand together as brothers and sisters and celebrate each other that we will truly become emancipated.

Dr. Deborah Bartlett

National and international consultant to private and governmental agencies, Dr. Bartlett, is the president and founder of the CEO Network based in the Bahamas. The CEO Network was established in 1997 to strengthen work ethics, raise levels of productivity and create a networking platform for economic empowerment. She is also the founder of the Economic Emancipation Empowerment Movement (EEEM) and Bartlett Media Enterprises (BME). Dr. Bartlett has started and supported initiatives for inner city transformation. She has created platforms for speaking engagements in schools, churches and civic organizations to promote and advance social outreach initiatives.

Dr. Deborah Bartlett can be reached by email at debbiebartlett2006@gmail.com.

PREGNANT OUT OF WEDLOCK

Kaynell Gould

One of our greatest gifts as believers is the gift of identity—knowing who we are and whose we are. When we are secure, there is less likelihood of us having an identity crisis and falling to the age-old tricks of the enemy. I came from a strong religious background and served in every available capacity in my denomination from childhood. We were taught right and wrong, and I knew the difference. Not just because of what was preached from the pulpit but what I was taught at home and through reading my Bible. I was the student in school people called on to pray, read scriptures, organize meetings, and sing. It was a joy to do this; I loved God with all my heart and knew I was called to serve him.

I always wanted a husband and a family of my own, and having a strong Christian upbringing, I did not want to be someone who slept around. So, at eighteen, I got engaged and married to who I thought at the time was my first love. We had two beautiful children during that eight-and-a-half-year marriage. It was a tumultuous one, and I suffered tremendously. My esteem was virtually non-existent as my husband continued to live his life as a single man without remorse. Not understanding at the time that the problem was with him, I questioned myself. Was I not good enough or attractive enough? Could I not satisfy him? Is that why he turned to others? The relationship finally came to a head; I did not have anything left in me to give and nothing left to help me fight the emotional abuse.

The Parade of The Fallen

Shortly after that, a young, good-looking, intelligent man began to show interest in me. I was taken aback initially; did he not know I was unattractive? Why did he treat me like I was lovely and worthy of love? He whisked me off my feet. His kindness was the healing balm I had sought with my husband and never received. I felt validated. Then, against my better judgment, we became intimate, and a pregnancy ensued. After the commitment, I began to see a different side of this man. The relationship became more controlling, and I couldn't see myself continuing down another path of abuse. Now that I was pregnant, I was even more terrified of what people would think.

What could I say to my mother, or the pastors, and my children? In despair, I confided in my mother, thinking she would be devastated and ashamed of me. Instead, she said, "What do you want me to do with you, throw you away? You are not the first to fall and you most definitely won't be the last." In her few words, my mother gave me the strength and courage to move on. By this time, I had been serving in church for several years in a leadership capacity, so I had to meet with my pastor. It was challenging, but I bore my heart to him. I was told that the church's policy was that fallen leaders had to repent in front of the congregation during the Sunday morning service. I shuddered at the thought of airing my laundry publicly but told them I would need time. I did not feel a release to do it that Sunday but would advise him when.

By the end of the meeting, I was more broken than I was when I came in. My legs could not take me to the parking lot fast enough, where I melted in my car seat, awash with tears. My heart was crushed. I knew I had done wrong, but where was the compassion and the guidance I needed? Did they not see that I was crying out for help? Instead, I was to be paraded like a wounded soldier from the enemy's camp to give my last words before being shot in the village square.

My phone rang as I wept inconsolably. A church sister was on the line asking me what was wrong; she had felt me in her heart. Understanding that I wasn't coherent, she told me to come to her home; I did. She embraced me, prayed with me, and listened with compassion. When her husband came home, he did the same. They cooked a meal for me and took me home. They never condoned my actions, but neither was I condemned. They promised never to leave my side, and they never did, even to the point of insisting I show up to church every Sunday.

Several weeks after meeting with the pastor, I graced the platform. I felt fear and shame initially, as I looked into the sea of people staring back at me. Somehow, a boldness came over me when I took the microphone.

I told the church I had fallen and repented. I asked their forgiveness and told them I did not want their pity, but their prayers.

As I wrapped up my apology, the senior pastor came forward, admonishing the congregation to embrace me and show me love. He cautioned them that they were not to gossip about me or treat me poorly, as many of them would have easily found themselves in the same predicament if they were not on birth control or had an abortion. That was the first and the last time I was shown love openly by the congregation—most of the people responded with the same attitude and mentality as the pastor I had met.

More than one life saved

A lady called the church, I was told, after hearing me share on Sunday. She said she had decided to come to church one last time, then her intention was to return home to commit suicide. When she heard me speak, she told the leaders that my testimony saved her life. Had I not waited to share when I had the peace in my heart to do so, I wondered if the dear woman would still be alive. A benevolent physician in the congregation who was known for his seemingly endless compassion was also moved by what I had to say and offered his medical services to take care of me and my baby. He did so free of charge from that moment to the delivery and beyond for my post-natal care. One of the leaders of the youth group in which I served pledged support and promised to help wherever I needed it. He became an angel on earth for those times I could not drive myself around. Despite the rejection, the stares, and piercing whispers, God had strategically placed people around me to help me on the difficult journey.

Kaynell Gould and baby.

Now with the precious baby born, though times were hard, I was thankful that I had her and loved and treasured her just as much as her older siblings. Not long after her birth, I was alone again without my daughter's father in my life. We were a family, and we were going to make it, even though there were times I barely had food to feed them and found myself going to bed without eating yet another night. I was grateful nonetheless as God sent people my way to help when the burden seemed heavier than I could bare alone.

A Ministry Is Birthed

Still resting in what I would call a hard place, the Lord spoke to me. He said he wanted me to share my story publicly. I immediately said no. It was too painful. How could he ask me to do such a thing? I knew, however that I had to be obedient and penned the first of three stories for print in a local newspaper. In my byline, I added my telephone number.

My phone rang day and night with ladies on the end of the line weeping and sharing their stories. They thanked me for my transparency as they felt a release of their heartache and shame in reading about me.

Then several men called to also thank me and commend me for my boldness. One of the men became a great friend and sowed into the group for many years.

When the Lord whispered in my heart to invite all of the ladies into my home for a meal and to share his love, I felt overwhelmed. How could I do this? I wouldn't know how to or where to begin. I shared this with my new friend. His side passion was cooking, so he told me to buy the food and set the date, and he would not only prepare the meal, but it would be his pleasure to serve my guests. I did, he did, and we all had an amazing evening, sharing, praying, and celebrating the goodness of the Lord.

Not very long after the group grew, and we were meeting more regularly. By this time, our group had become a vibrant ministry called Single Mothers United, with a board of seven women. We would arrange clothing drives for the ladies and their children. The donations were passed on to them free of charge. Initially, we were in the church I attended, but I was asked by the leadership to submit my ministry to one of the other ministries already established in the church so that the efforts were not duplicated. I yielded and did so. There were some leaders who were still uncomfortable because of my history and did not feel I should be allowed to operate. As very little attention was given to the members of my group, they eventually stopped showing up. It was at that point the Lord told me that I was released to take it back, which I did, and we began to flourish again for several years even reaching as far as Freeport, Grand Bahama.

We held seminars, conferences, and meetings to empower women and their children. Not long after, changes took place in the ministry once again with the marriage of three of the board members, the passing away of two others and the relocation of another to another country. Notwithstanding the effort placed on empowerment seminars to help the ladies get their lives on track, most placed their emphasis on the free items we were giving. I saw it and was grieved by the turn of events. However, I was grateful that the Lord had given me a release to cease our operations until further notice.

It was during one of our conferences that I met a lady who was to become my pastor. She poured life into me. She built me from the inside out. In the moments when I needed it, she was there supporting, encouraging, and feeding me the word. There were times I was forced to look at myself, check out my life, and do deep introspection. What were the parts of my life I needed to give to God? If there was unforgiveness or bitterness, I had to release it. It was obvious that there were some broken things in my life, and I needed to have them restored. This dear pastor walked me through the process. During this season of my life, it also became clear to me that I had to stay pure before God, so I opted to raise my children without complicating the process with relationships. It was after all the relationships that got me in the predicament that I was in.

A Time to Apologize

While on vacation, I was led by the Lord to go on a fast. One day as I was laying before the Lord in prayer, he told me to get up. He was not hearing me as I had unforgiveness in my heart towards my former pastor. My unforgiveness had gone on too long. I replied, explaining to the Lord that my pastor had hurt me tremendously. He insisted that I do the right thing in any event. I got up and made an appointment to see the pastor. As I sat in front of him, I recounted our meeting two years prior. I told him that I had not come to him expecting him to celebrate what I did, I came expecting to be pastored. I came expecting him to love me, not what I did. As a pastor, my pastor, who I served under in various capacities faithfully for many years, he had tossed out all my good with my error in judgment, an error I needed to be counseled and mentored through.

It was as though my character and service all those years meant nothing. I told him that rather than counsel, I left his office wanting to commit suicide. His eyebrows raised. I told him that he made me feel worthless. He sighed. I told him that I had come to ask him to forgive me for holding him in my heart all this time. I asked for his forgiveness, and he accepted, telling me that if he didn't have respect for me before, which he did, he certainly did now. I left his office with a weight lifted from my shoulders. I had not realized that unforgiveness could be such a heavy debilitating load. I felt the healing hand of God on my life through releasing what was held in my heart.

I have a burden for women who have been wounded, who are broken and feel as though their lives are on pause. Those women caught in an ongoing cycle, needlessly repeating their mistakes because they lack information that would free them to live overcoming lives. Women who are having multiple children for multiple men and taking out their frustration on their innocent children.

I have a burden for women who in their frustration, believe that denying their children's fathers' parental rights is hurting the fathers when in fact, it is destroying their children, who don't just want their fathers, but need them. Those ladies have not gotten past the hurt and pain despite the men apologizing for what they had done to hurt them. Ladies, you don't have to live as a hamster on a wheel, doing the same thing repeatedly but expecting a different result. God not only wants to heal your brokenness, but he has a beautiful life set for you and your children if you would just take his outstretched hand. What he did for me, my sisters, he can surely do for you.

Kaynell Gould

A banker by profession, Ms. Gould has served in the industry for approximately 34 years. She is an engaging motivational speaker and minister of the gospel who has served in various Christian ministries throughout her lifetime. Ms. Gould currently serves as an Elder at The Embassy International Ministry in Nassau Bahamas. She is the mother of three adult children, and the grandmother of four.

In addition to ministry, Ms. Gould has a passion for preserving the heritage of the Bahamas and has captured the essence of a generation of people considered to be peace-loving and gentle through her book Emerald Isles of the Azure Seas, which can be found in the Bahamas at All Seasons Gift Center in Palmdale.

She can also be reached at ladykaynell@hotmail.com.

THAT OLD MAN IS DEAD

Delvonne Duncombe

I grew up on the island of New Providence in the beautiful Bahamas. My father's parents were descendants of Andros and Eleuthera, and my mother's parents were descendants of New Providence Island. Daddy was the oldest of eighteen children, and I was the oldest of all the grandchildren. Being the oldest grandchild, I grew up with my father's youngest siblings and often was treated as one of my grandmother's children. I remember the days when she would cook and have the bowls lined off on the counter from oldest to youngest; the funny thing with that was the older you were, the more food you got, especially meat. Being the youngest meant that I hardly got meat and would often have to eat from my grandmother's plate, who we affectionately called Ma.

Ma And Dad's House

Those days were great; they were days when manners and respect were the cornerstones of training in the home. My grandparents,

Ma and Dad, lived on the corner of Market Street and Andros Avenue; I spent many days, nights, and summers there. My grandparents guided me throughout my early childhood. Dad was a preacher and a well-known evangelist. His belief in God and his desire to achieve made him a stern disciplinarian and a model of excellence for his children. Ma was a praying woman. She never worked a job, yet with eighteen children, she would always bellow her work was never done. I remember the summers we would spend at their home with our morning beginning with 'morning preez' as we would call it, a spoon of Buckleys and honey and a spoon of Vaseline. I never quite understood what that was for, but it was not up for discussion. Next, we would be sent out of the house and allowed to play in the yard with each other, our neighbors and friends from neighboring communities who would all come to the yard just for fun and frolic.

This is where it all gets interesting. This is where my story begins and gets a little scary. It all started at the five-bedroom single-story structure on Andros Avenue. Before I tell my story, let me say that I have forgiven all who hurt and took advantage of me as a child. I love them unconditionally and never once lashed out or acted indifferently toward them. As I look back and assess my past from a new and enlightened perspective, I now understand why I did some of the things I did in my youth. I also realize the importance of parents providing a healthy environment for their children where they can holistically express and be themselves.

My parents provided that environment for me when I was home. My father and mother did their best to help me maximize my potential to become a successful young man. Their parenting method was authoritarian, which at the time gave me the structure and discipline I needed to navigate through life as an adolescent and later as a man. Daddy taught me many essential principles about life, one of which I would never forget. He often said, "If you want to know, you should ask. If you want to be better, you should seek knowledge." I can still hear him today, "Delly, knowledge will never find you; you must seek knowledge." Mummy was also a disciplinarian; she was small in stature but always taught me the value of manners and respect and how I should put God first in all that I do.

Hearing all of this, one may wonder how something as heinous as molestation could happen to someone in such a home environment that my parents had. I have no answer to the how and why, only to say it happened to me. I think I was about six or seven when it first happened. It was not until I was about eight or nine that I understood that something was wrong with what was happening with several aunts, and by the age of ten and eleven, I think I knew what was happening but did not have the courage to stop it or even speak out against it.

This sexual abuse led to years of promiscuity as a child, a teenager, and even a young adult. I believe that because of the molestation, I had become desensitized to the dangers of premarital sex and engaged in many promiscuous acts.

The Age of Innocence

I believe that adults are responsible for protecting, nurturing, and loving children under their care. At no time should anyone strip a child of their innocence. It epitomizes selfishness. Children are impressionable, and their minds fragile. Emotionally, they are delicate flowers that, under the sun's scorching heat, can wither and die for lack of shade. Imagine what it must feel like for a six-year-old to be fondled consistently during baths, not understanding what is taking place or why what is happening is happening. Now imagine a seven-year-old child being made to touch the private parts of someone they trust and who they have been given the responsibility to nurture and protect.

Can you imagine how that child, whether a little boy, like myself at the time or perhaps a little girl, which is also commonplace, feels when they are made to look upon the body of an older man or woman, not entirely understanding what is happening? At such a tender age, a child does not know the purpose of their bodies; they

69

don't understand what they are looking at and being drawn into. The emotional fallout is tremendous, the fear and scars are lasting, and only the love of God could bring wholeness back to that individual's life. For some, wholeness never comes; they grow up to be broken individuals, never truly understanding who they are and always seeking to justify what happened.

Well, I was one of those little boys fondled by caretakers. Worse than that, family members—aunts, who were supposed to ensure that I was safe. Instead, they violated me; took away my innocence. They caused me to always question who I was and why I was a candidate to have this physical and emotional pain inflicted upon me. At six, I didn't know better; I could not be held to account; I thought it was all a game; after all, I did get a cup or a baggy afterward. As a child, I thought it had its benefits. After the treats, I believed it was ok; I was confused. This continued for about two years, and the confusion increased for two years. Why was I being made to do things that no little child my age should have to do? I kept silent because I was told it was our secret, and I liked the treats, but I didn't understand the seriousness of the tradeoff. I was innocent and unaware. Nobody told me what I was doing or what was being done to me was wrong. I was the victim of abuse both sexually and emotionally, and though disturbed, I was clueless that something should or could be done to stop it from continuing.

This Can't Be Right, I'm Confused

At eight years of age, I realized what had been happening to me just couldn't be right. I thought I liked girls. Will they let me touch them the way my aunt touches me? Is it ok if I ask them to come into a dark room with me so we can kiss? I was confused. Why did I get in trouble for lifting a girl's dress? My aunt lets me lift her dress and look at her undergarments. Why couldn't I take my private out and show it to another girl? It must be normal; she is of the opposite sex. I was confused.

70

For me, the next couple of years were so confusing. I wanted to do to others what was being done to me; besides, it felt good in a weird way. I thought maybe I could do it with someone else, and they would enjoy it too.

I always kept the secret, which never bothered me because, at the age of innocence, I did not know better. But for some strange reason, my body reacted when I saw girls I liked. I wanted to show her that I liked her by touching and fondling her. I wanted to let her know that it would be our little secret and that I wouldn't tell anyone ever what we would be doing. It didn't take long to realize that what was happening was not normal, simply because I got in trouble often with teachers, which resulted in me being scolded or punished for this behavior. The question for me was, why was I confused? This was not adding up, and yet I kept the secret. I liked the candies, the ice cold 'cups,' the 'baggies,' and now the salty I was getting.

Maybe I Like It!

I was ten years old; I had a friend in the neighborhood that let me touch her, we kissed, and she touched me. By this time, only one of my aunts continued to touch me, but our touching had elevated to rubbing our private parts against each other. I was learning, so I believe that it was helping me to do so much with my friend in the neighborhood. I thought it was awesome, and I still kept my aunt's secret. I didn't even need the candies and the other goodies. Aunty just had to let me know where to meet her. She gave me the signal, and I met her at the location. I couldn't deny that it felt good. Though my mind is questioning my actions, my body is enjoying the sensation. Maybe that's why at eleven, I was not avoiding her.

At twelve, I was looking for her to ask if she wanted to go and do 'da ting.' I liked it; this is why I tried to insert my private into my friend's private part because I wanted to see how it felt. Perhaps that's why I hid in the closet to watch my uncle have sex with his girlfriend. My little life was becoming unraveled. Sexual promiscuity was the order of the day for me, and I wanted to know more, feel more, and do more. My aunt was not enough, so I stopped looking for her. I was like Columbus: I wanted to explore the new world. The question for me at thirteen was, what will this new world present?

The Secret Is Still Safe

As a young teenager, I engaged in sexual activities fairly early: lots of masturbation, the occasional fondling of females, and intercourse a couple of times. Because of my early introduction to sex through incest, I was on a destructive path. I got involved in gang-related activities and started to smoke marijuana. Being exposed to sexual activities at an early age skewed my view of the world. Oddly enough, my secret was safe, my parents never knew, and I functioned as a typical adolescent in their presence. If you were to ask my mother about me, she would have a glowing statement of how mannerly and disciplined I was. The secret changed me; it caused me to be able to hide the truth about who I was and live in the shadow of who I wanted people to think I was. I became good at it; at home, I was the model son, at school the class clown, and on the streets, a gangster—oh, and how can I forget, in the church, a spirit-filled believer. I now know that my secrets kept me bound to a wrong view of myself, a view that in no way reflected the challenges I would have gone through.

When Purpose Prevails

Today, despite my troubled past, I was able to transition by the grace of God to becoming a devoted father and loving husband, the senior pastor of a local assembly in the Bahamas, a naval officer in the Royal Bahamas Defence Force, and a mentor to countless youth within my country. I accept that I am the sum of all my experiences, but I also know that I did not have to travel that road. Despite the journey, I can help others who have been on a similar road to what I was on. People who were taken advantage of by family, friends, or even strangers live in a silent hell.

Although my secret is out, and I am better today than yesterday, not everyone can say the same thing. As adults, parents, and even caregivers, we must do whatever we can to ensure that children are taught early about not allowing people to touch them sexually or inappropriately. They need to be kept safe and have open lines of communication with us, and they need to know that it is wrong for anyone to ask them to keep a secret from any wrongdoing.

Lt. Commander Delvonne Duncombe

I am resilient; I am strong because my strength came from the Lord. But what about the children still caught up in this kind of situation? Or what about you who are reading this? Were you a victim or a predator whose body betrayed you, and now you feel condemned or guilty about your participation and do not know how to break the cycle, get rid of the pain, or embrace a healthy future? You can do it. You can lay your past to rest. You may need help, but you can get through this to live the extraordinary life God has for you. I did it, and now you can too.

Lt. Commander Delvonne Duncombe

Lt. Commander Duncombe currently serves as the Director of the Defence Force Rangers, the nation's only military youth program. He is the president of CHANGE Organization, a youth training, development, and mentorship program. Lt. Commander Duncombe is also the Senior Pastor of Whosoever Will Discipleship Center in Nassau, Bahamas. He holds a Bachelor of Arts Degree in Psychology with a concentration in Child and adolescent development and certification in Moral Reconation Therapy.

Committed to excellence in all that he puts his hands to, Lt. Commander Duncombe is also a skilled computer technician, dynamic leadership speaker, trainer, life coach, and a certified member of the John Maxwell Team. In addition to his background as a physical fitness training expert, Lt. Commander Duncombe is an avid basketball player. He is also the author of Journey to Greatness, A Life Guide For Youth & Young Adults & Their Parents. This character development book of life lessons is designed to close relational gaps. He is married to Shamica née Johnson and is the father of four amazing children. Lt. Commander Duncombe can be reached via email: delvonned@yahoo.com

LIVING A DOUBLE LIFE

Darnella Diggis

My uncle Ned was generally a quiet guy. He wore life loosely as though he were young and single without a care in the world. But if there was a gathering and boisterous laughter filled the room, you could be sure that Uncle Ned was at the center, dazzling onlookers with his wild tales. However, he spilled the beans when he drank alcohol, letting his deepest thoughts run wild like a chicken escaping a coop. Daddy used to say, "If you get a man drunk, angry, or his passion stirred, you'll hear exactly what is on his mind." This was true of Uncle Ned, who had an entirely different disposition when he was sober. It didn't matter that Aunt Julia heard his stories when he was drunk, he didn't remember, but she did, and she kept them close to her aching heart.

My Early Impression of Marriage

One of the things Uncle Ned used to say was, "Marry a young gal; keep her busy and in the dark! The simpler she is, the better it is for you!" The people roared with laughter knowing that Ned did indeed have a wandering eye and a trail of indiscretions with young ladies who had no exposure to the things of the world. Everyone knew that Julia was many years younger than him. Aunt Julia listened quietly. She was caged, had no money, and nowhere to go. I felt sorry for my aunt. She had become broken and bitter, the two things I vowed would never happen to me. I knew I would be different, I would be better, and my husband would love me completely. I would out-serve him and out-love him, he wouldn't be able to escape my love. I believed that and nobody could change my mind on the matter.

I lived a sheltered life with my sister, brother, and parents. Daddy died just before I went to college, but when he was alive, he treated Mom like royalty—such love and respect. I wanted the same kind of relationship. Marriage was what I dreamt of—I wanted my knight in shining armor to love me as Daddy loved Mom. When I went off to college, I met Mike, a young jock in my art class. He had an irresistible charm about him, his eyes sparkled, and I was mesmerized by him. Mike could have had any of the other girls on the campus, but I was flattered because he chose me—he called me a Bahamian beauty. I was a 5'6" brown-skin gal, well-endowed with large breasts and buttocks, a typical island girl who the American guys considered exotic.

I Believed It Was Love

Despite my Christian upbringing I melted when Mike made advances toward me. I loved the attention he lavished on me. He told me I was the only one for him and I believed him. It didn't take long for Mike to charm me right into his bed. It was my first time but not his—I was a well-planned conquest.

Mike was excited about the pursuit but wasn't keen on having a relationship. His idea of a relationship was sexual engagement, which became too frequent for me, but he assured me it was the norm. When I found out that I was pregnant, Mike accused me of seeing someone else, claiming the child was theirs and not his. Heartbroken, I went home to have the baby. I was ashamed of the rejection but loved Eric, my beautiful healthy son. Mom kept Eric while I completed my college education, and I was grateful.

Two years later, I met Jimmy. He wasn't anything like Mike. He accepted Eric and asked me to be his wife. We had so much in common. I was a set designer, make-up artist, and budding actress. Though he had a mentorship program for young actors, Jimmy was a playwright and director who traveled to New York and Los Angeles whenever the opportunity availed itself. During our courtship, Jimmy and I were never intimate. After we got married, we were rarely intimate. I thought nothing of it. Jimmy was my best friend; we were busy making waves with our careers. So much so that we were dubbed a power couple among our peers.

Several years into our marriage the criticisms began. At first, they were subtle remarks that gnawed at my self-esteem. No matter what I did, there was a comment. I became extremely self-conscious.

My breasts were too big, I waddled instead of walked, my style of clothing was unattractive, my laugh was goofy, my hands and feet were unattractive... I began to wonder what was right with me. Why didn't he like my hair? Why didn't he say so before? What about my clothes? Do you really have a problem with how I sit, talk, and smile? Rather than arguing, I did my best to improve, asking God to help me to be a better wife and friend to the man I loved and committed to for life. During my private prayer time, rivers of tears flowed from my eyes—I wanted to improve, I had to be the woman he wanted. After crying and lamenting before the Lord, I got up and served my husband, preparing his meals and taking care of him the best way I knew how. Whatever it took, I was committed to improving.

Whenever I left the house, Jimmy wanted to know my every move. I was flattered at the attention. I thought despite his unkind words, he really cared for me. He was like the satellite in a spy movie called the *Eye in the Sky*, always tracking my whereabouts. My exact movements had to be known. When he called, I happily told my friends, family, and even people serving me in the store that it was my husband checking on me. I let them know that I had a man who loved me and wanted to make sure I was safe, especially with the heightened crime on the streets. Granted a few looks were awkward, but I chalked it up to jealousy: those girls wished they had a man in love with them as my Jimmy loved me.

Then came the unsettling feeling in my heart. I had been praying for so long for God to direct me, to fix me. I was sure that I was the broken one. Something was not right, I confided in my best friend tearfully, who suggested I do some investigative work of my own. She needed to know if I could handle what I might find out. I knew I just needed the truth; we were already heavily invested in our marriage of almost thirty-five years. My friend had a plan and I followed foot to foot behind her to achieve it. Hours after we implemented the plan, notifications began to roll in when Jimmy returned from work. To my complete shock, I discovered that my husband was not only addicted to porn, but he was gay. My world began to crumble. Now I knew why he wanted to know my every move. I was duped. I had become the girl Uncle Ned joked about, the girl who was always busy, naive, and clueless about what was going on right in front of her. I said it would never be my lot in life, yet I was in a worse predicament than Aunt Julia.

A Time to Think Things Through

I decided that I would take a trip. I needed to clear my head. Strangely enough, I noticed Jimmy didn't want to know my every move while I was away. As long as I traveled, he had the run of the house, and he could lavish himself on porn for days on end—or, as I discovered later, he could bring his lovers into our home—into our bed. The reality hit, and it hit hard. I was never his wife; I was his cover! When I returned from my trip, I sought legal counsel. My lawyer recommended that I not tell Jimmy how I knew, only that I knew.

To my surprise, he was relieved that the secret was out. He hated having to fight his inclinations every day of his life. Jimmy was on a roll, his words slid from his mouth like a dagger from a well-greased sheath. Jimmy wasn't angry or drunk, I had touched his passion. He claimed he never loved me; he had always been attracted to men; tall, slender, good-looking men. He called names, some I knew, and most were young boys being mentored by him. Others were older guys who were married like he was, and yet another group were those who lived an openly gay lifestyle.

The married men ensured their wives were friends so they could have an alibi to be together. I couldn't believe what I was hearing. Jimmy gushed like a broken dam.

I was nauseated, but like a deer caught in the headlights of an oncoming truck, I sat frozen, unable to move or speak until he called the name of our close friend who had recently died of AIDs.

"You mean you had sexual relations with Greg and didn't have the courtesy to tell me so that I could get checked?" I was livid.

In his usual dismissive manner, Jimmy said he didn't see why he should. I felt sick to my stomach. How could I have been so trusting? What else did this man do that I should be aware of? I wondered about my son. Had he been safe? My head spun. If only I could get Jimmy to repent. If it were a demon, I knew we could resolve the issue if Jimmy wanted to be free. We could get rid of it. Our pastor had cast out many demons before, so I knew he could set him free. Jimmy didn't see it that way. He said he now knew that God was not real and there was no such thing as hell. I realized a deceiving spirit had taken hold of him. He chose to believe a lie to allow him to continue living a debased lifestyle guilt-free. With his newly claimed status as an atheist, he could do what he wanted and not be burdened by a conscience.

I shared our conversation with my friend. She insisted that my focus needed to turn from Jimmy to my well-being. I needed to have myself medically checked out. She used a testing center in Tulsa years before when she was in college, we could make an appointment for me to get checked and return home in several days. After a battery of tests for STDs, I did not have AIDs, but I contracted three other sexually transmitted diseases, two of which were treatable.

I was angry and became bitter. The bitterness moved from my head through my body like venom. By the time I realized that the bitterness was affecting me more than it was Jimmy, it was too late—my body was sick, and if I weren't careful, I would let a cold-hearted man be the death of me. I didn't want to die; I wanted him to feel the pain he inflicted upon me. Unfortunately, the pain backfired. I decided I had to let the hurt go. It was difficult because of the flood of memories that triggered thoughts, which triggered more thoughts until I was wallowing in heavy despair. I wondered who else knew that I was being duped by this man. Now, in addition to the pain, I was battling shame. The cycle started again, unraveling fears and tears by the bucket. I had to get off this merry-go-round. I had to forgive Jimmy because it was the right thing to do.

I Needed to Be Free

Wanting to be free, I surrendered him to the Lord and felt the weight lift from my life. I finally had peace in my heart. By this time cancer had taken hold of one of my breasts, it had to be removed and I chose to have chemotherapy. With all the expenses and no one to help me financially, I couldn't afford to live anywhere except in the home I built with my husband. I told myself it was for a short season, he in one part of the house and I in the other. We were civil and civility eventually turned into being cordial. I didn't want to renew our relationship and neither did he, but I had to establish some ground rules while living there. His lovers were not to darken that door while I lived in our house. My son, now married and living on one of the Family Islands, did not know what was going on until the divorce was finalized. Eric was angry and disappointed and wanted to do his stepfather harm, but eventually calmed down. I never told my siblings the reason for the divorce, and my mother had passed many years before. I was literally alone, except for my old friend.

Jimmy's Accident

After recovering from surgery and coming to terms with not being able to change my husband's lifestyle, Jimmy had a terrible car accident, leaving him wheelchair-bound and unable to work or care for himself. After his medical expenses, he was almost penniless. His lavish lifestyle of catering to his lovers had placed a dent in his finances. With no work and no insurance, I felt compelled by the love of Christ to take care of him. I heard about another lady who had gone through a similar situation. In her case her husband left her because she was sick and he didn't want to waste his life on a dying woman, so he moved in with his lover. Shortly afterward, he got sick, and his lover felt the same way and booted him out. The wife, who had recovered, took him back in and cared for him until his death despite how she was treated. When asked how she could, she simply noted that it was a supernatural grace she could not explain.

Now I was in a similar situation as the only person who was by his side. He had family, but none he could call on. I could now relate to the lady who cared for her sick husband. God had also given me a supernatural grace to take care of the man who had inflicted emotional abuse and had taken advantage of my kindness for so many years. Each time I did something for him, he wept. He knew I could have abandoned him to his fate. I came to expect the full-fledged bawling of a grown man who had become a shell of who he had been. I watched the cruel, pompous nature dwindle. There was a softening in his demeanor. For the first time in his life, he considered me a friend—perhaps his only friend.

The surgeons were able to save his legs, but whether he would walk again, only time would tell. Jimmy has reconciled his relationship with the Lord and is growing in his faith daily. As for me, I'm free. Challenges still come at me from left field, but I've learned when to pray and when to duck and pray. I also realized that no matter what we are going through in life, it is not hidden from Christ. The Word assures us that He, God, is with us always, and it also says he will never leave or forsake us. I now know that to be true. Though things may get rough at times I am comforted knowing that the God of Heaven loves me with unshakable love and wants his best for my life. One thing is certain—I have overcome, and I will live a bountiful life despite the devastating plan the enemy orchestrated against me.

Darnella Diggis

Ms. Diggis resides in the Bahamas. Though she still assists her former husband in his recovery, she is also a student and a full-time business owner who is committed to living a life without regrets.

BROKEN AND BETRAYED

Sherry Tyndle

When my husband Ken and I were married, it was a dream come true. I was the bright-eyed girl who married a minister and would have the happily ever after story. I never considered myself a complicated person. I loved the Lord and always enjoyed the simple things in life—like taking care of my husband and children and the beauty of the rising sun as I drank my first cup of coffee for the day. I loved Ken, and I placed his desires and well-being above mine. I believed and still do believe that love gives; it is selfless. Unfortunately, I came to find out that Ken and I did not share the same view. Ken did come to our marriage with well-concealed baggage, but I was also far from perfection. I was young and inexperienced, and my identity was not entirely as formed as it could have been. Nevertheless, the happily ever after ended abruptly. Not for lack of effort, but for my safety and our children's, I had to walk away with literally what I could fit into a suitcase while my husband was off the island.

Return Where?

It was the most gut-wrenching feeling to know that God was leading me back to my husband after being divorced for almost three years. If anyone knew how difficult it was for me to live through a turbulent marriage and finally come to a place where there was some semblance in my broken life, it was God. I stayed close to him. He knew my every thought; he saw what I went through, and it was his shoulders I cried on daily. Why would he want me to return to Ken? I felt like Jacob wrestling with an angel for an answer, but I wasn't as strong. I also considered the prophet Hosea who God asked to marry a prostitute in the Old Testament. Hosea was heartbroken and humiliated times over—could God really want me to do such a detestable thing as remarrying my ex-husband? Did he forget what my children and I went through? It was difficult to wrap my head around what I thought he wanted me to do.

Instinctively, I knew I had to forgive Ken for his part in our marriage failure and did so almost routinely. Notwithstanding giving him to the Lord and praying for his soul, I battled hideous thoughts and horrifying dreams about Ken. I was embarrassed to speak about how I wanted to cause him physical harm. My self-esteem was battered; I felt I had little value. Ken was a master of turning the tables to make me feel small, useless, and crazy. Although relatively calm to look at, I was in deep anguish. The man had emotionally abused me for so long that I felt like life had been sucked from me. I was alive for our young children, who were also unfairly affected by Ken's behavior. Ken came from a wealthy family, but we were not initially a wealthy couple. He worked hard, was favored with high-paying projects, and his family was indulgent and often yielded to his requests. Soon we were living in a beautiful house in a gated community. Most people would think that the house alone would bring joy to any girl's heart, but I'll be the first to let you know that money, cars, or even a large luxurious home won't satisfy the longing in your heart for peace of mind in marriage. My house was my prison. Don't get me wrong: it was beautiful inside and out with tremendous views. It didn't have bars or locks that kept me in, but emotionally I felt as though it was rigged with impenetrable steel doors that kept me from seeing the light of day.

We Looked Good on The Outside

Between my young children, hunkering down in prayer, and keeping our home clean, I had little time for much else. The emotional toll had affected my body, and I felt like I was running close to an empty tank. Meanwhile, Ken prospered in his career, despite prophetic warnings that he needed to get his life in order or he would lose it. The money continued to flow in, but he was not keen on using money on his family.

During the summer heat, the air conditioner could not be turned on until he was there. Instead, we had to open the screenless windows and doors and hope that the bugs stayed out and a cool breeze would blow through.

We were a cashless family before debit cards existed. I was afforded a modest car to drive in and provided with a charge account at a local gas station when I needed gas. When it came to groceries, Ken gave me a signed check. I went to the store twice per month. Even when he traveled, I was not left with cash. Ken, on the other hand, spared no expense on himself. He drove his dream car and dressed in expensive clothing while we dressed in clothes my mom bought us from the Goodwill thrift store. Still, I served Ken, loved him, and learned his hobbies so that I could spend more time with him, as his job kept him busy.

Issues Compounded with Drugs

I found out about Ken's drug habit fairly early in marriage. I don't know if I was too naive to recognize the problem or if my hands were just so full as a young mother that I couldn't see the forest for the trees. What I couldn't ignore was a candid conversation I had with one of my husband's friends. He was bothered by his participation in a weekend-long drug escapade at our home with

Ken when I was off the island. Ken was a great actor. Initially, you couldn't tell what was going on, but eventually, he got careless and left a trail of his indiscretions behind. Some he brought into our home.

It was not unusual to have out-of-town sleepover guests in our home. I wasn't always thrilled about it, but I was hospitable, nonetheless. When a frightened young man who came with a so-called male minister confided in me that the minister was insistent on him engaging in sexual behavior in my home, I was beyond angry. I let Ken know that I did not agree to such sordid activities in our home, especially with our children around. He pretended not to know anything about it, but the company he kept and the lewd stories he told of what his wealthy friends were doing with their kids were concerning.

By now, Ken was letting his guard down and openly watching pornographic videos in our family room, leaving a trail of evidence behind himself. Instead of being sorrowful, he told me I was not a necessary part of his life. He found porn more enjoyable than having sexual relations with me—I could not satisfy his dark fantasies and did not want to. This was not the start, nor was it the end of our journey through a difficult marriage. Ken's warped sense of rightness took him through alleys where he hung with street thugs to satisfy his drug needs. At times he went to the opposite end of the spectrum to hobnob with the elite to do drugs and satisfy his perversions.

After abandoning our kids and me for almost two weeks with only the name of the city he was flying to, the single check left for our groceries was exhausted, and there was no food in the house for the children. I was desperate and ashamed. I reached out to a friend who took me to the grocery store so that I could feed my family. She had also been my resource for my son's clothing since we could not shop for clothes, and it would have been months before my mother's return.

Was This the Last Straw?

That night I reached a low point. I called every hotel in the city listed in the telephone book asking for Ken until I found one at two o'clock in the morning. My gratitude for finally finding him was short-lived when I was connected to his room, and a man answered the phone. I could hear the sheets rustling as he slid the phone to Ken. My stomach made its way to my mouth. I felt sick, but I kept my cool. Still in a daze, Ken and I spoke. He was surprised and annoyed that I had called him. I could hear that the man was in bed with him. It was clear what I had to do. With no money of my own, and financial assistance being turned down by Ken's family, friends came to my rescue to buy tickets for my kids and me. I was determined to leave before Ken returned. A lovely lady sat next to me on the flight out of Nassau, innocently inquiring why I was leaving such a beautiful place. I could not contain my grief any longer. With tears streaming down my face, I confided that I was leaving my husband, who no longer wanted to have a family. The stranger said she was a Christian and gave me a book to read, promising to pray for me.

Now that I was getting my life together with my kids and my new job after being free of Ken, his family reached out to me. Ken had fallen on hard times. The house was in a state of disrepair, and he had almost lost it to the bank. They (his parents), had to step in and save it. Ken had reverted to the days prior to our marriage when he sold his body and lived on the streets. Thankfully, they were able to get him into rehab. Though it tarried, the prophetic word about him hitting rock bottom came through. I felt like screaming in anguish, but nothing was coming out. The family said Ken wanted to apologize to me and wanted me to call him. I did, but I was hesitant after not hearing a word from him or even an inquiry about our children in more than two years. Ken did sound sincere, which is a novel thing for him. I accepted his apology. One phone call led to the next, and soon we were on friendlier terms. Then Ken told me in his usual pointed way that he'd like his family to be together again. I was taken aback. What possessed this man to even consider asking me to take him back? This time he promised we would make it work; he would be the godly man he was supposed to be from the beginning. Every ounce of my being cried, "Noooooo!" I refused, remembering with great clarity the deep pain and humiliation. I did not want to rekindle a relationship on that level with him.

My feelings were still raw, and the thought of being intimate with him again sent chills down my spine. After leaving our home, Ken had several different lovers move in with him including a man, his drug supplier. There was just too much hurt and so much dirt. I felt flooded with the waves of humiliation from the past. How could I ever give myself to a man I now considered repulsive?

Nevertheless, I listened. I always wanted to be in God's will no matter how I felt about the issue. God saw the whole picture. He knew the end from the beginning. It was, after all, his grace that kept me in the first place. I agreed to take baby steps with Ken but made no promises. He did seem to have changed. He was kind and thoughtful and even seemed patient when I was ready to throw in the towel. After months of deep counseling and working through anger, fears, and concerns, Ken and I were remarried and accepted a post in full-time ministry with me at his side. We eventually returned to our home in Nassau, and I vowed never to leave again.

Several years in, Ken's arrogance began to poke its head through the doors of our home again. By this time, I was pregnant again, and it was not an easy one. I struggled to get things done, walking up stairs to get to our bedroom. Ken's heart was hardening once more, his business was growing, and he was making lots of money. Instead of asking me what I needed, knowing that I was having a difficult time, he demanded more of me even though I could barely get out of bed some mornings. The children, now older, were not comfortable around their father—they dreaded his coming home and hated the idea of spending time alone with him. They heard his condescending tone and dismissive attitude towards me at home when we were alone or had guests.

A New Gift to Our Family

Soon our baby was born. I wondered how someone so precious could be birthed at such a troubling time in our lives. The child brought our children and me so much joy. I began to see how it was worth having the baby despite the trauma. Ken refused to give our baby any attention. He barely looked at him. He refused to watch him while I showered. I don't believe it was because of the child. He was innocent and could hurt no one. Ken's behavior had become erratic again. The older kids were traumatized, had nightmares, and begged me to leave again. I was adamant: I was going nowhere.

His sexual indiscretions were rampant, and he didn't even try to hide the evidence on his clothes. If I voiced my concerns, Ken knew how to talk me down. He said I was insecure and jealous, and if I tried to leave again, he would have me committed to an insane asylum.

I didn't want to go, I promised to make it work no matter what, so I spent more time praying for Ken and asking God to help me become a better wife and mother.

Despite my prayers, I could not ignore what was going on and became concerned for our well-being. My husband had friends from the underbelly of society and would not think twice about harming us. It was one of my children's fears, who had recurring nightmares of the same. Upon a friend's suggestion, I hired a private investigator to figure out exactly what he was up to. That was one thing that had changed from the first marriage; I now had access to our bank account. The list of activities was enough to convince me that it was time to leave again—this time, I had to plan more carefully.

With the older kids visiting family abroad, I began packing our personal belongings and shipping them out. When the bank alerted him of the unusual spending, he questioned me about it. I told him something from the top of my head that he bought, knowing that I was prone to help others. Of course, it angered him, but that was the last of the significant spending except for my ticket. I was ready and only awaited the release in my heart to go.

The timing had to be right. It was God I believe, who directed me here, and I was awaiting his instructions for my release to leave. When the day of our departure came, only one person knew. She drove us to the airport, where we said our goodbyes, and I hastily boarded the flight. Despite loving it so immensely, I was never so happy to leave anywhere, even though I had wonderful friends.

I've wondered why I had to go through that time with Ken for years. In telling my story, I'm convinced that God chose to bring good out of a terrible situation with the birth of our youngest child, who is undoubtedly Heaven's gift to our family. While I am not bitter or angry anymore, I have no regrets about leaving Ken. I would venture to say that it was perhaps one of the best decisions I made. Who knows what might have happened to the kids and me if I had stayed? My kids are young adults, and they all love the Lord. In all the years they have been separated from their father, he has not once offered them genuine support in any form, which does not surprise us. But he has connected with them once or twice to find a way to stir up mischief.

Stronger and Better Prepared to Face the Mountains

Like most people, we still have our mountains in life to scale as we come to grips with the trauma inflicted on the kids. However, we are grateful to God for bringing us out of our Egypt, knowing that Heaven sustained us throughout the ordeal. Over the years, I wondered what I could have done differently for a healthier marriage. One thing is sure: loving your spouse is not the only ingredient for a successful relationship. I loved mine, and it didn't make a difference. In addition to the love factor, their character and knowledge of God's word and his plan for marriage, along with the wisdom to implement his guidelines with understanding, is what it takes to have a successful marriage. Dr. Myles Munroe commented on marriage being like an omelet, saying that both eggs had to be good. He was right. My advice to anyone who asks is to work on being a good egg. That means know God, develop yourself, strengthen your character and never look for someone to complete you. Being a whole person before you are married is perhaps the best gift you can bring to your marriage.

Sherry Tyndle

Ms. Tyndle is a seasoned lay minister who has dedicated many years to restoring hurting individuals and broken families in her community.

REJECTING THE DARK ARTS

Philippa Melvyn

I knew my mother had two children, my older brother and me, other than a miscarriage she claimed to have had before my brother was born. I never questioned it. Almost sixty years later, standing in a packed church, a man who I'd never met before, a foreign prophet, had called me out to minister to me. I was familiar with the spirit realm, having experienced good and evil, and was committed to good. The prophet was not an unexposed man. He had left his home in Africa to be free from his grandmother, who was also heavily involved in witchcraft. He could relate to what I was going through.

"How many children did your mother have?" he asked when I stood to face him.

I answered, "Two." That's when he corrected me. The third he said, was sacrificed. His comment took me by surprise, but by now, I didn't put anything past my mother. For the last several years, I had seen her in action and had found out that she was also involved in the death of my only child. I had even seen what she had done to my father after he made a comment in front of her that she did not like. Daddy was okay one minute, and after she placed her pointed finger on his shoulder to reprimand him, he became extremely sick. That's how she operated.

It is unfortunate how many people would choose not to believe my story. Many have convinced themselves that witchcraft, voodoo, obeah, Santeria, and the like do not exist. Unfortunately, when they find out that it does, they become fearful and succumb to it instead of taking a stand against it. You don't have to be fearful if you are a follower of Christ. When Jesus commanded his disciples to go out in the book of Matthew 10:8, "to heal the sick, cleanse the lepers, and cast out demons," he would have been in error if demons did not exist. In many instances, Jesus and his apostles cast out demons. How do you cast out something that does not exist? Yet, all over the world, what was considered an evil only found in Africa is prevalent in Haiti, Jamaica, Cuba, the Bahamas, Brazil, and America. In fact, all over the world, especially in Europe, where sadly, it is a growing fad. Yet so-called Christians either believe or pretend that witchcraft does not exist and rather than learn how to walk in God's power, they buckle under the weight of their problems. They do not really understand that their God is all-powerful, all-mighty, and nothing can defeat us if we surrender to him. Then we have the other extreme, those who falsely believe that demons outrank God. That's a lack of knowledge.

The prophet continued, "Your mother had someone spit in your mouth when you were a child." By now, I was on the floor; my head was reeling. I later asked the Father about what had been said, and he showed me who it was and where it was. The prophet had told the truth. So much had happened, and now the pieces were starting to come together. All I wanted was to jump from the roller coaster I seemed to be strapped to for so long. Had someone told me that Mummy was involved in witchcraft when I was younger, I may have denied it, but of late, there was nothing I would put past my mother. To strangers and even my brother, Mummy was a soft-spoken, sweet lady who used to teach Sunday school; unless you ruffled her feathers in a bad way, she turned her volume up. That volume wasn't just sound. It came with effects—deadly effects. Mummy had a long line of devilish people in her family. Her father was deeply involved in witchcraft along with his second wife, not Mummy's mother; she had passed away when Mummy was a teenager.

Her grandfather, who was my great-grandfather, was a fisherman who hailed from Jamaica. Great-grandfather was a high-level warlock who migrated to Long Island, where he lived with his pregnant wife and son.

Both father and son were killed in a storm at sea, leaving my great-grandmother to raise my grandfather. My grandfather, the pastor of a church, was said to have inducted all but two of his children into the occult.

I Did Not See

For many years, it seemed that just about everyone in my family knew the family's history and their evil shenanigans except me. I was raised in a home that was a marriage of convenience. As my father told the story, he and my mother lived across the street from each other when they were growing up. Many a night, he would come home from work at sea with his father to see my mother on the front porch. She had been put out and made to sleep on the porch yet again. After having seen this and being tired of his home arrangements, he suggested to my mother that they get married. It was their way of escaping their parents' homes. There was no love between them. In fact, after marriage, they continued to live separate lives—he went his way, living a double life, and she went hers doing the same. Despite this, Mummy did her best to provide meals for Daddy. It was one area she was committed to, much to my annoyance at the time, as it often made us either late for church or unable to go. I had a deep love for the Lord despite my family's history. Mummy was the Sunday school teacher, and other than the general bickering between the two of them at times and my intense dislike for him, I thought our lives were normal.

The Unusual Visitors

After my parents divorced, Mummy lived with me. Her bedroom was across the hall from my own. It seemed she didn't sleep at night; I could hear her talking to someone. When I asked her about it, she claimed people were coming into her room. At first, she claimed they walked around and searched through her clothing, but soon they were trying to force something into her mouth. Initially, she resisted, but eventually, she yielded to her dark visitors. Night after night, I could hear her chattering away and sometimes screaming. One day I told her we needed to get her help. We were Christians after all, and did not need to accept what was happening. Each time I suggested it, Mummy resisted. On the one hand, she would say yes; on the other hand, she wanted to know who was coming and when, but she would not be there. It seemed odd to me. I decided not to pursue it.

When I needed to borrow Mummy's car one day, she casually suggested that I ask Satan for one. I thought perhaps she was joking; she was not. I reminded her that I served the Most High God and would never do such a thing. As time passed, I noticed my attitude towards Mummy changing. I was fine until she was close by, and I would become unusually irritated. I snapped at her for what seemed no apparent reason. After she commented on it several times, I realized that it was something I had to pray about. I asked the Lord why this was happening. He showed me in a dream. I spotted Mummy in the dream, and when she saw that I had seen her, she tried to hide, but it was too late. She was clearly in cahoots with the demonic beings in the dream. She now knew that I knew what she was into; she had sold out entirely to Satan. Nonetheless, she was my aging mother, and I felt it was my responsibility to take care of her, which is what I did.

Losing My Son

I had a brief marriage. During that time, I had two miscarriages and the birth of my son. He was close to Mummy. I was naive about the extent of her influence in his life. They became inseparable, and soon he was like putty in Mummy's hands. Unable to handle the darkness that invaded his life, my son took to using drugs. He died, and I was heartbroken. At the funeral, I was approached by a man, a well-known pastor who was a friend of my mother. They had been extremely close for years. He was not only a pastor but the principal of a local school. He approached me and thanked me. I was at a loss; I didn't know what he thanked me for until some time later. As my mother's partner in crime, I later found out that he thanked me for allowing my son to be sacrificed. Sacrificing a man was more valuable than a woman. I felt sick. I had nothing to do with it and would never have agreed to such a thing.

A family member who had known about the family dealings years before I did came by to visit and telephoned the relative they knew was responsible for following Mummy's instructions. While placing the call on speaker for me to listen in, she confronted our relative about her deadly activity. The person merely said, "Do not tell Philippa. But I need you to come over so we can discuss it." The information was now out, and Mummy was in the house. I was sure she heard the conversation. Later that day, Mummy said, without me asking, that she had nothing to do with my son's sacrifice. It was the first time I had heard her mention the word sacrifice; she could have easily said death.

Having Mummy living with me was becoming increasingly difficult. She said people were coming into her room at night. I advised her to tell them not to come, but Mummy's behavior was changing even more, and at times an unfamiliar pungent odor was coming from her. I noticed that it happened just before some dastardly deed of hers was set in motion. It was the scent of witchcraft. Every step of the way, I dug deeper into the word, asking God for his guidance. Each time he gave me a scripture or showed me in a dream what I was to do. On one occasion, I had had my fill of Mummy and the demonic intrusions in my house, which often disrupted my sleep. I decided to visit a friend. She was a strong Christian who often heard from God. I knew I could trust her. She braced herself to tell me that the Lord said that I should pack my mother's suitcase and move her out of my house.

One of Us Must Go

My friend was surprised that I had agreed to do it without putting up a fight. She knew I had been long-suffering with Mummy. I told the Lord I would do better and pack two suitcases, and I did. My brother agreed to take my mother, which minimized the troubling manifestations in my home. As she left, Mummy quipped that I probably wouldn't be having the uninvited guests in my house anymore. It took a while, but I realized that in trying to be civil to Mummy on the phone, she was keeping me on the phone to send witchcraft my way. After each call, there was a demonic intrusion of some kind. Sometimes they were in the form of spirits that would leave when I commanded them to in the name of Jesus; other times, they were snakes throughout the house, which I also dealt with. It never failed. After each call, there was an attack of some sort to my health or home.

Before Daddy passed, we reconnected. I put the past behind me with the resentment I felt toward him and got to know him all over again. Daddy was able to fill in many of the missing pieces in my life concerning Mummy. He was disappointed at where her life had spiraled to. But he knew her family's history and saw the trend. I realized that no family is without issues, but my own was far greater than I was able to bear anymore. I wanted to be free of anything knowingly or unknowingly passed down to me. A friend suggested I see a deliverance minister. The lady was sincere and walked in the power and authority of the Lord Jesus Christ. During the deliverance session, the minister asked me about two of my children. She was seeing them as she spoke with Jesus. The little boy was asked if he had been sacrificed, and he nodded a yes. I named my son before he ran off to return to Jesus. The little girl was a few years older, and she too said that she had been sacrificed. I also named her. For the first time in my life, I felt free as the minister broke demonic strongholds from my life.

One evening as I was working on a project in my home, I sensed an evil presence in the house. I knew someone was in there with me. I asked the Father for his help. He opened my eyes to see into the spirit realm. As I walked into the living room, I saw it filled with people. They had parted to allow me to walk through. Moments before the Lord had given me a scripture, 2 Timothy 1:7: "For God has not given us a spirit of fear, but of power and of love and of a sound mind." I didn't realize that I would need it so quickly, but I did. I shouted it boldly. I told them to leave at once as I did not fear them. I called on my angels to escort them out, and they left. Occasionally people who visited my mother while she lived with me would come to see me after I had her move out. They claim to be touching base. These people feel as though they are doing the right thing to patch a broken relationship without even taking the time to ask what has transpired. Though they may not be directly involved in witchcraft as my mother is, by association, they have become carriers of darkness as they never fail to trigger the dark realm with their visits, leaving a trail of mishaps in their path.

God is All Powerful

The fight is real, and it continues against the forces of evil, but what I have learned throughout this terrible experience is not to be fearful. To thrive, you can't have a superficial relationship with the Lord, and you cannot be weak-minded. You will have to know who you are in Christ and that you really do belong to the Father. An essential part of being victorious is knowing the word of God—it is a tool of warfare. The demonic realm does not respond to my voice. It responds to the word of God spoken through my voice. Many readers are experiencing an invasion of the evil realm in their life but don't know what to do. Don't stay silent. Ask God to direct you as you walk towards your freedom.

Philippa Melvyn

Born and raised in Nassau, Bahamas, Philippa Melvyn spent her early career in the hospitality industry. She is a local artisan who creates handmade apparel and handbags. Ms. Melvyn hopes her story will help those bound by irregular dark dealings in their families to seek help to experience the peace they richly deserve.

THE SHOTGUN WEDDING

Anna L. Lewis

When my grandfather says that you are marrying the man you're dating, that's it. End of story—all you can do at that point is set the date, especially if you were seven months pregnant. In his house there was no backchat; he spoke, and you obeyed. At least that's how it was for my mother when she became pregnant at eighteen. My mother was a normal teenager, fresh out of high school in Nassau and brimming over with life. Her father, my grandfather, was a hardworking contractor who lived in a small community in the eastern district of New Providence with my grandmother and their six kids.

Everybody knew my grandfather was strict and laid down the law with his children. He had high hopes for Mummy and kept her close to home. She was, after all, not just the second child but the first daughter of his union with my grandmother, a career nurse. In those days, Mummy spent much of her time at church. She was always involved in the youth meetings like many of the kids her age. Mummy didn't share her story with me until later in life after some of the stories began to come to the fore. She was pregnant with me and forced to marry a man who was not my father. By the time of our conversation, she was a changed woman and a minister of the gospel.

Nonetheless, it was clear that she was somewhat embarrassed that I had found her little secret out. I could see the burden lift from her shoulders as I repeatedly told her, "Mummy, it's okay." Those three words had become a healing balm to the woman I had to forgive for the wounds inflicted upon me throughout my life under her roof. Mummy needed to be released from the guilt and shame she had carried for so long.

Who's My Daddy?

The road to marriage and family was rocky. What was meant to be joyous was painful. Mummy and I had a history neither one of us wanted to repeat. I understood her pain and confusion and realized that it all started when times were different and parents weren't as open with their children about the ways of the world. It's not an excuse; it's just how things turned out. Nobody told her, and though she found out the hard way, she didn't know how to tell me or talk to me. Mummy was an inexperienced youth having a child without anyone guiding her.

In any event, over time, the pieces of her life came together, with me an unwilling participant, smack in the middle of it. It was when I was thirty that I was made aware of some of the background stories that unfolded in Mummy's life. This helped me to understand why Daddy was so harsh and sometimes extremely unkind to her. He did begin to settle down after one of my brothers challenged him not to hit her again. Not knowing the details, I also encouraged Mummy to leave the abusive relationship, but she never did. I don't recall Mummy retaliating to his verbal and physical abuse; instead, she spewed the venom toward me.

It all began innocently enough: a naive young girl, as I said, fresh out of high school, riding on the church bus with its driver, a man many years her senior. I don't know if Mummy felt compelled to or what the exact details were, but she and the bus driver became intimate, which was considered taboo, if only for the age difference. Though it may have happened several times, and he had a girlfriend who recently gave birth to his daughter, theirs was a brief encounter. When Mummy realized she was pregnant and could not keep the information from her parents anymore, her father was told. Before doing so, however, Mummy said she informed the bus driver, who gave her some money to terminate the pregnancy. Thankfully, Mummy chose not to.

During this time, Mummy began seeing an upcoming young man who was closer in age to her. They too had been intimate, so her father, wanting to cover the shame he felt the family would experience with a teen pregnancy out of wedlock, ordered a shotgun wedding. The atmosphere at the wedding was so thick that someone said you could almost cut it with a knife. Daddy's family wanted answers: why did their son have to get married so quickly? It was obvious that Mummy was seven or eight months pregnant. To show their discontent, the family played Percy Sledge's song, "Take Time to Know Her." The man I grew up calling Daddy was forced into a marriage he did not want.

When I was born a month or two later, all eyes were on me. Daddy and his family's greatest fears were uncovered: I had zero resemblance to him or anyone else in his family. He was of a lighter complexion and here I was, a beautiful, darker-skinned baby.

I was ready to be loved and embraced by my parents and the new world I had made my grand entrance into, only to be placed in the hands of two scared, hurting people, one of whom felt like he had been duped, just like his family said.

When I was eleven, my parents moved to Andros. By now, Mummy was an auxiliary nurse, and Daddy worked for the Ministry of Education as a security guard. The heat in their relationship was rising. I could not understand why Mummy vented her anger on me. For years I curled up just wondering what I had done and how I could stop the constant physical and emotional abuse directed at me. As I grew older and more children were born into our family, it was clear that I was the odd child out. My siblings were clearly a blend of my parents.

The Anger That Led to Abuse

It wasn't unusual for Daddy to become heavy-handed with Mummy. He was not inclined to trust her. Whenever she went out, he was suspicious, especially if it was to another settlement. He just wasn't buying her story and was quick to accuse her of cheating on him. I don't know if she did, but I do know that it was a domino effect. He got angry, lashed out at Mummy, and she in turn took it out on me. There were several times she had me pinned to a wall shouting expletives with a knife to my stomach. Mummy said she had brought me into this world and would take me out of it. The picture was burned into my mind and weighed heavily on me throughout my life. Though burdened, I didn't share my heartache with anyone. I tried to drown my sorrows with fast company and parties and became involved sexually in my mid-teenage years. Rather than talking to me about my reckless living in a calm manner, Mummy listened to unfounded gossip, leaving me feeling burnt once again by accusations that were far from true. On one occasion, she told me in anger that if I were pregnant, I should abort the baby. I didn't understand why she said it then, but I do now: she was afraid that history would repeat itself and the pain would continue.

At sixteen, I had given my heart to the Lord and enjoyed serving in my local church. I was industrious and sought opportunities to earn money to supplement some of my school needs. Although active in my church and loving the Lord despite my dwindling wayward activities, I worked part-time at my cousin's restaurant and bar. When the church I attended heard about it, I was no longer allowed to participate in their programs. I was crushed. I felt as though I was being rejected on all fronts and couldn't understand why. Why was I singled out when others my age were openly visiting nightclubs? It was another crushing blow that left me wondering why life was so unfair to me. I eventually left the island and returned to Nassau, hoping to find a better life and employment. I believe not being in the house, coupled with my brother not tolerating Mummy's abuse, brought much-needed calm to the house.

Another blow was dealt, however when I was about to get married. Mummy came and walked me down the aisle. I wanted my daddy there, but he refused to come. The excuse Mummy gave at the time was that he was not feeling well, but I later found out that he suggested that my real daddy walk me down the aisle. Both my parents have passed away, and though I would have loved to have a conversation with Daddy to let him know that I knew about the situation and understood his pain, it was too late to do so. I wanted him to be free as Mummy was after our brief conversation. Unfortunately, that was not to be since I found out after his death. I'm older and wiser and have chosen not to hold grudges or judge people for the decisions they made in their lives.

Meeting My Biological Father

I was thirty when I met the bus driver. It was at a funeral, and he introduced himself to me as my biological father. When I asked him about what happened, he said he asked Mummy what she wanted to do about the pregnancy but did not get a clear response. He said it was the last time he heard from her and understood she had moved to one of the Family Islands and later had a daughter.

After questioning why I was wreaked with emotional pain for so many years and why I was born, my heart cry was answered with the scripture in Jeremiah 1:5, "Before I formed thee in the belly I knew thee; and before thou camest forth out of the womb I sanctified thee, and I ordained thee a prophet unto the nations." It was painful knowing how my life started and even more painful how I was treated by the people I thought should love and accept me the most.

But now, my eyes are open to the truth, I am here, and I have a purpose. And although it was not in God's plan for me to go through what I went through, he takes even the bad things in life and makes them beautiful. The death I felt that I experienced in my childhood was like seeds being buried to spring forth new life. My tears watered the seed, and through my journey, I was able to learn how to express the gift of poetry that was to be a part of my future and the future of those lives my writing is supposed to touch. I wrote this poem during one of my darkest hours.

Cries Within

I'm screaming, I'm frightened
When will it all stop?
The cries I heard from my mother
Now STOPPED.
"Is she dead?"
"Did he kill her?"
Is all I could ask,
While hoping and praying,
This fight would be the last.

Do you think of the kids
When your anger gets away?
Do you hear our quiet whimpers
Or do you just brush it away?
Teacher says we should love each other
Our neighbors, family and friends.
So why is it that in my house
The fighting never ends?

Am I the issue?
Born of a father, not sure...
Compared to my siblings
Each day, my looks, my walk
My talk.

I hear the whispers of grandma
As we play saying,
"She really doesn't look like my Joey!"
And I wonder daily,
So, it is me, it is me!

My small mind starts…
I'm not loved by anyone, anyone
Then my tears start.
See Mama was very young when
She had me.
And back in the day once you
Were pregnant you were forced to marry.

Am I a bastard?
Does anyone care?
The father I thought was mine
Is no longer there.
The fighting has stopped,
To Mom's relief, I'm sure.
He died from a heart attack.
Life, I know…

Many years since passed
I am adult by now,
Still feeling unloved, lost
Wondering how…
How can life be so mean

To one who didn't ask to be?

Still wondering...

Searching...

Does anyone love me?

Who would have thought that the little girl who cried herself to sleep, who tried to run away from herself, would run right into the heart of God? In running to him, I found the gifts he gave me and have since written two books of poems that bring healing to the lives of people in need of encouragement, people who want to give up and feel that their lives are hopeless. People who have been abused or perhaps are abusers need to know how others feel after their unkind words and gestures. I don't believe that God caused my pain, but he used the gray clouds in my life to wrap his silver lining around them to encourage you and me.

Anna L. Lewis

Anna L. Lewis has a gift for turning pain and other life issues into poetry, as laid out in her two published books. Anna and her husband Jeremy are young entrepreneurs on the beautiful island of Eleuthera in the Bahamas who operate a fishing charter, a car rental company, and other business ventures. When not penning her thoughts to paper Anna enjoys singing, fishing, baking, and traveling. Anna's poetry books merge her world with that of its readers. The books are available in paperback and Kindle on Amazon.com, or by contacting the author via her Facebook page or by email at anna81lewis@gmail.com.

HUNG BY THE TONGUE

Teri M. Bethel

Growing up in a large family, I was number three of six kids; it was amazing. As children, we didn't have to wait for friends to come over; we always had company. We had an enormous yard with amenities and several dogs and cats on hand. I knew the yard well from an early age. It wasn't just because I spent many of my days climbing trees while foraging for the biggest, juiciest fruit or playing hide and seek or cowboys and Indians with my brothers. Nor was it because our parents lived their sporting dreams vicariously through us, causing us to excel in swimming, basketball, and tennis. No, it was because I regularly trekked the yard with Mummy as she walked me up and down, teaching me my times tables and spelling. I don't know how she did it as a working mother with five other children, but she made time for me. I was a skinny little girl with the long, straggly plaits and bundles of energy, and though while in public I was painfully shy, I loved to entertain my family. Having them laugh with me was always better than them laughing at me.

Where Do I Fit In?

I was surrounded by clever, confident, and talented siblings. For some reason, I didn't fit in any of those categories, and when the comparisons began, I froze. I was in the spotlight again, not for any outstanding achievement, however—quite the contrary. I was in the spotlight because I was the dumb child, the sibling I had been told on many occasions, who would never do well in life. That was the beginning of my inner turmoil, locking myself away, hoping to move from the failure status to invisible. I wanted to disappear. Granted, I still loved my family, and everyone knew that one way to put a smile on my face was to play music. It was as though the music turned into a happiness gel-like substance that permeated every fiber of my being. Mad, sad, bad, or glad, it didn't matter how I was feeling; when that music kicked off, I was the queen of the poppy show.

That's when the laughter began, and the family seemed to be knitted together until the next squabble. The disputes ranged from whose time it was to wash the dishes to who encouraged another to put a frog in the housekeeper's handbag to who helped to place the patio furniture and exercise mat in the twelve-foot-deep swimming pool. In all cases, the disputes somehow found their way in front of Chief Justice, Sir Daddy. That didn't usually entail spanking: Mummy was the "go get me the switch" parent, and Daddy was the "give me fifty laps in the pool" one. His discipline was usually multi-purpose.

I felt like I experienced a brain freeze when it came to school. It got to the point where I didn't want to try to do better. I believed my family and didn't want to be in another altercation. If they said I was dumb, there was nothing I could do to change that, even though my teachers thought otherwise. As early as I could remember, my report cards read, "Teri could do better if she tried." In my little mind, I couldn't try. Trying to do better would mean I would make my family out to be liars if I did well. I wasn't daring enough to travel that route. Instead, I just prayed and asked God to make me vanish. I rushed through everything I did. If I was in a tennis tournament, fear gripped me so fiercely that I hit the balls in the net just to be done with the match. I couldn't bear all eyes being on me. My family couldn't figure out what the problem was. We played tennis almost daily with each other and Daddy's friends, and though I wasn't in the same league as our youngest brother, I was pretty good at it.

Teri M. Knowles

My mother used those opportunities to socialize me. She would often tell me to look in the eyes of the person I was speaking to and address them by their names; she claimed not to do so was rude. I did when she was around but quickly slipped back into my shell, not wanting anyone to look through my eyes lest they see the depth of despair I was feeling. I learned how to camouflage my inadequacies as I grew by performing with false confidence.

That meant on the outside, things looked great, but on the inside, I was still lost, fearful that I was one step closer to becoming the failure I was told I would be.

Growing up with three brothers, I learned how to fight—it was fight or be tormented by the two oldest pranksters. Daddy insisted that the older girls join our brothers in self-defense classes, so I was no pushover, but no kicking or punching prepared me for the fight I encountered into adulthood.

To Boarding School We Go

We were elated when the opportunity arose for the four older siblings to go to boarding school. I was eleven, and we considered it another adventure, a new frontier for the overly energetic, mischievous bunch. Our destination? The girls went to a convent run by Irish nuns and the boys to a Catholic school run by Irish priests, both in North Wales, perhaps an hour from each other by train. The nine-hour non-stop flight from Nassau to London, followed by an hour's drive to the train station, a five-hour or so train ride to Rhyl, and what seemed like an hour's ride to the boondocks of Denbigh in a mini with a heavy-footed nun, flying through the dark narrow road felt like I was living in another time. Daytime at the convent was a beautiful sight to see. Behind us were spectacular green pasture lands sprinkled with gorgeous shade trees and dew-soaked sheep hidden beneath mounds of wool and, in the distance, snow-capped mountains. On the street side, a scary, foreboding wall wrapped its way around the entrance, shielding the imposing red brick building that housed the chapel, kitchen, dining hall, and upstairs sleeping quarters for most of the borders and the nuns.

For many, my sister and I were the first people of color that the town had ever seen. Being followed into the bathroom in the early days by dorm mates on the third floor wanting to see where my tail had been cut off was becoming stale. By the end of the first term, most had stopped asking about the tree house we lived in like Tarzan's. Thankfully the photo album Mummy sent to help us through the inevitable homesick days proved we were humans. Despite the cultural adjustments, I made wonderful friends. Being a picky eater, most food like porridge, cold cereal, eggs, watercress, and cucumber sandwiches never made it to my lips. I ate crisps (potato chips) doused with ketchup and hot sauce whenever I had the opportunity, and though I was never a fan of bread, sliding a banana through a hotdog roll-shaped bun and flooding it with sugar was often my go-to breakfast. This eventually led to some weight gain and, of course, textured freckles—you know what I mean, pimples, the dreaded zits which my brothers were quick to say looked like guava seeds scattered across my face. Puberty was not fun for an already insecure child.

The following year, the fear did not leave me. The new adjustments just compounded what I was going through. The condemning thoughts and insecurities, the challenge of trying to tame or comb my thick, wild hair that had long outgrown being straightened, and not having the best relationship with my sister who dished out insane punishments like writing a one page essay on what was on the inside of a ping pong ball because I did not stand when she entered the room, as was the custom for seniors.

The dorms were icy cold, despite the overworked radiator at the end of the room and the blanket-thick underwear that rose above my belly button. The dark wood corridors and squeaking floors leading to the single toilet on our side of the second-floor dorm seemed like miles away. I had to walk past the nun's sleeping quarters, and the winding wooden staircase that looked like it should have been in a horror film to get to it. The setting was far from what I was accustomed to. The lone toilet at the end of the narrow passageway was shared with three dorms. There was a separate tub room with a single bathtub for what could have been more than twenty girls whose beds were lined off, separated by a single nightstand and a curtain for privacy, much like a hospital ward.

Our personal closets, possibly the width of a twelve-inch broom closet, were on the wall opposite the foot of my bed. It was cold, and we did not bathe daily as we did back home. Our bath times were scheduled two or three times weekly. In the interim, we washed from our bowls by our bedside, having towed a line to collect the water and relieve ourselves for the morning. We called our twice-daily routine the sign of the cross. That was washing the face, the southern private, and the two armpits before going to chapel and then to breakfast. Chapel was early morning before breakfast and after study hall in the evening and was as enjoyable as a tooth extraction.

During this time, mustering the courage to ask the nuns questions seemed futile. You read and accepted; you didn't question or seek understanding; that was considered cheeky. I desperately wanted to connect with God but thought he had gone on strike or only spoke to the nuns in their holy black attire. As Anglicans or non-Catholics, we walked several miles to a nearby town every Sunday to get to church. Though surrounded by the most beautiful landscapes, it was seemingly void of people younger than Moses.

The trek was made two by two in sunshine or snow. Apart from perhaps two others from the town and the ancient priest, the service housed less than a handful of us girls dressed in our smart green skirts, yellow collared blouse with a necktie, and blazers trimmed with red and a hat and on snowy days a long, hooded green cloak and sometimes wellington boots.

Brigidine Convent Boarding School.

Photo Credit: Janine Quinn

We were required to write home each week, and every now and then received wonderful care packages of native treats as did many of the other students from their families. There were no cell phones back then, but we did get to speak to our parents for a few minutes every week, at least for the first year; my older sister had the dominant personality and had more lengthy conversations than I did. My pleadings to God increased each night as I tearfully begged him to take my life. I awoke to a pillow wet with tears almost every morning, my face stiff with hardened mucous, and being a bed-wetter, my four-inch mattress on a wire frame was saturated. I was too fearful of crawling from under a warm comforter to travel through what seemed like a spooky cold dungeon. It only added another layer of fear and insecurity to my dilemma. With no one to turn to, I felt more alone than I had ever been in my life.

Classmates at Brigidine Convent.

Despite my challenges, I made friends with most of the students, although still somewhat confused by the statements of a classmate who openly shared her mother's reasoning on why black people were black. She claimed it was simple. When God told everyone to go to the river to wash themselves, the blacks were the nasty ones who washed only their hands and feet. Our punishment was to remain stained as a constant reminder of our plight. Despite a few of these misinformed people, who I remained cordial with, I was grateful for the kindness of the Matron, a white South African, who treated me well despite having to air my bed regularly for several semesters, and my P.E. teacher whose kindness and faith in my gymnastics, tennis and netball abilities had no limit. Some of my classmates who I've recently reconnected with invited me to their homes for weekends and holidays, making me feel as though I was a part of their families for the four years I was there.

Those were days I will never forget. I saw how siblings were caring with each other and how in one of the homes, in particular, my friend's father treated his wife with such love and respect it impacted my decision to consider marriage when Tellis proposed to me. One of my closest friends was a brilliant student and musician; she took me and another friend under her wings and coached us through math and science classes.

From Hopeless to Hopeful

Four years later, my brothers and I were transferred to a co-ed high school in Orlando, Florida, where we met individually with the school's principal. That became a pivotal moment in my life. The principal. was the first person to tell me that he had high hopes for me and that he had heard of me and my accomplishments. His little pep talk had me wondering who he was talking about. It could not have been me, yet it was. I left his office smiling, and for the first time in my life, I felt as though I really could achieve great things in life. In retrospect, I believe he was referring to my athletic ability as I did exceptionally well playing netball and tennis at Brigidine. At the time, I somehow took it to mean my academics.

My mind shifted, and the dark cloud of gloom that followed me for most of my life began to break away, allowing the light of the day to penetrate. I became more confident and started asking questions and applying myself. Before the end of the year, I was considered the MVP of the girls' basketball team and had made it to the honor roll for the first time in my life. I stayed on the honor roll my entire time there, and good grades were my lot at the university I attended in Tallahassee, Florida. When the high school principal invited me to make extra money cleaning his house as another young lady of color was doing, I respectfully declined asking him why me and not one of the white girls or his daughter. I didn't have a problem cleaning. I just didn't like the idea that they thought just the black kids should do it.

Your Kind Are Maids

My major was Journalism and Mass Communications, which I chose to impress my parents. Though I had not gotten into the thick of the coursework, the thought of it was as satisfying as a bowl of sawdust. I had made much progress in my classes, but I was still flying low, not wanting to be seen. That's when I decided to transfer to Los Angeles, California, to study interior design. In one of my classes, a project to interview an interior designer in the city was pending, and my grade depended on it. When I was finally able to make an appointment and drove to a wealthy neighborhood almost two hours away, the black housekeeper peering through the cracked door, looked at me quizzically, wanting to know if I had the correct address. I had never seen someone looking so oppressed and fearful.

She eventually guided me to a dark living room whose drapes were drawn, where I was confronted by an older white woman who told me that my kind had no right to pursue such a career. We were supposed to be maids and gardeners and nothing more.

The older woman laced into me for what seemed like an eternity. I felt weighed down and unable to move. I was angry. It felt like my energy had been sapped. I had seen some racism in England and several times had watched the Klu Klux Klan (KKK) dressed in white hoods drive through the school's campus in Orlando. I even

119

had opposing teams refuse to shake my hand after a basketball game because I was black. The blacks in the primarily black university I attended in Florida and the multi-racial college in Los Angeles also showed prejudice because of my lighter skin, but I had never ever encountered such hatred as I did with this lady.

I sat unmoved initially. Partially because of pride—I was a Bahamian, and we were free to be what we wanted to be and did not need anyone to tell us otherwise. That was a thought coming from one who had been fearful of living her life. I also sat through the abuse, knowing how important the interview was for my grade. However, with the constant verbal battering, a different kind of fear gripped me. I didn't know who else was in the house of horrors or if I would be allowed to leave in one piece—I couldn't count on the timid maid to save me. I was suddenly overflowing with tears, knowing nobody knew where I was. The lady railed into me, trying to destroy all sense of self-worth I had mustered. When I was finally able to leave, I wept all the way home, feeling like a massive foot had stomped me to the ground with no hope of me ever getting up. Had my younger brother not pulled out his Bible and encouraged me to read it, I may have quit school. The next day I spoke with my instructor, who was understanding and worked with me through the project.

A week or so later, I handed in another assignment due to a different instructor. The theater-style classroom was packed as he commented on the work handed in. One, he claimed, was superior to the others. "This is what I expect!" he bellowed as he stood waving my assignment in his hand. The instructor insisted that he meet the student responsible for this stellar piece of work at the end of the class. When I introduced myself to him, his face dropped a mile. Refusing to speak with me, he abruptly handed me the papers and shooed me away from his desk. It was too late. He had already let the cat out of the bag: my work was good, and my self-confidence was restored despite having to fight for the right grade for every assignment that followed.

It was much later that Daddy shared some of our country's history with me. He said it was not to stir anger or hatred, but it was important to know where we came from as a people in order to move forward in life with wisdom and not repeat the mistakes of the past. He told me that in his youth, a black person could not walk on the sidewalk if a white person was on it. You would have to move or be forcefully moved. Those were the times he lived in. But in our home, things were different. We were never taught one ethnicity was better or more important than the other. The shade of your skin did not determine your worth, regardless of what people had to say. Hearing my story was not a surprise to him. It was horrible, but not a new mindset.

The Graduate

With my confidence on the mend, I returned home a graduate of the Fashion Institute of Design and Merchandising, portfolio in hand. I wanted my family to see that I had made it. I was not the failure some thought I would be. My future looked bright, and I was thankful for the financial support I received for the ten years I had spent away at school. I knew that it had been a sacrifice for my parents, and I wanted to make them proud. Soon after returning, I raced to see my father to tell him once again how grateful I was for the opportunity he had given me. He was with a friend. He got up, embraced me, and turned to his friend to introduce me. I wasn't the daughter who just graduated; I wasn't a child he was proud of; I was the dumb one, he told the stranger. My heart sank. Despite so much happening, nothing had changed from their perspective. The words spoken over me time and again in different forms from various family members had reared their ugly heads once more.

As I adjusted to returning home, I desperately wanted to be mentored. I needed so terribly to be told, "This is what you can do; let me guide you. Or you can make it; you're going to be okay!" For years I groped in the dark, trying to make headway but faltered instead. My older brother had turned his life around and told me about the church he was attending. I was disheartened when he said that I was not a Christian as I thought—at least not according to the Bible's definition. I had been a religious, part-time churchgoer—I wondered if that was why I felt dry spiritually for so long. I did not have an authentic relationship with God. I was offended, but I needed to know the truth. The church we had been going to as a family was dry and boring. I took flack when I left that church and made my way to my brother's church. Several weeks later, broken and feeling like I had hit rock bottom, I cried out to Jesus and asked him to take charge of my life.

I was tired of trying to make life work—I was failing miserably at it. As I lay in the passageway of my apartment, I wept bitterly. It had been a while since I cried; I thought I was tough and over the tears. Even my mouth had toughened up. I operated in retaliation mode: You hit me, and I'd slice you with my words. I didn't like who I had become. I felt dirty and broken, I needed to be cleansed, and I knew only Jesus could do that. When I finally got up from the floor, having confessed my sins and repented, I felt a weight lift from me, and a presence bathe me like liquid love. A new Teri was born—I was a baby learning what to feed on and realized my need for having a relationship and not a religious experience.

The new Teri began writing poetry; it was a way of expression and emptying myself of the hurts I felt and saw. I compiled and published my poetry initially under a pen name. My writing was riddled with errors, but it was therapeutic. I pressed on to improve my craft. My family questioned me, wondering if I were indeed the writer. Years later, I became one of the better writers in the family and the only published author who has now published twenty books of multiple genres. Before his passing several years ago, Daddy told me I did well; I had surprised him. He was proud of me and the family my husband and I had raised.

He loved it when our children came around and shared stories of his past failures and successes and how proud he was of the young men they had become. While ailing, Daddy asked that his family photos be enlarged and placed around his room so that he would always be able to see us. They were too small, so I created a picture book of his family and friends, starting with his parents to his grandchildren. We loaded it with tributes from his children as we celebrated his life with us. Daddy loved the book and had me read and reread the tributes to him as his eyesight was poor, even with glasses and the help of a magnifying glass. When I was done, he told me to place it somewhere prominent for everyone to see how much his children love him. I then realized that he was fragile, just like the rest of us, despite his tough demeanor.

Several years later, after Daddy had passed, I sat on a plane with Mummy; she said, "Teri, who would have thought you would turn out this way? I am so proud of what you have accomplished because you were one dumb child!" I laughed because she had always denied saying or believing that before, but now it was out; old age had loosened her tongue. I really believe that my situation started innocently and snowballed out of control. My family did not set out to hurt me, but like sticks and stones, words can hurt, and if you're not careful, they can even kill.

I've often wondered about the limitations we have placed on ourselves and others by speaking negative words rather than words to encourage and build up. Apart from my situation as a child, I have found that some people have difficulty attributing value to others simply because the devaluing of another makes them feel important and takes the spotlight off their limitations. With these kinds of people, you can't convince them to appreciate or accept you. You just have to reject those words and neutralize the assignment to marginalize you and learn to appreciate yourself. Then you move on to being around people who will celebrate you.

It also became clear that I had to forgive those I felt had marginalized me to progress. The unforgiveness and fear brought untold torment leaving me to waste time rehashing scenarios and possible outcomes that only made me bitter while others moved on with their lives. It didn't matter what people thought of me, it was God's view of me that counted, and I had to learn to love myself and others, which was not an overnight process. It was late in the game, but I understood that we couldn't all be the same. Our purpose and giftings are for a reason. In any event, words are powerful, and they do matter. They release blessings or curses in a person's life, but it's up to us to accept and watch them flourish or reject them and ensure they die.

Teri M. Bethel

Teri Bethel is an author, ghostwriter, literacy advocate, newspaper columnist, podcaster, and publisher. In addition to her writing, she is a professional Interior Designer and a self-taught artist. Her love for art and the creatives led her and her husband Tellis to enter the light industries field to manufacture hand-painted resort wear and her distinctive line of Teri Monique hand-painted designer handbags.

Mrs. Bethel seeks to encourage and empower people to be their best through her relationship books and novels for children and adults. She and her husband have served in various aspects of ministry, including Marriage, Youth, and Women's Ministry. The couple has two sons.

Mrs. Bethel's books are available in New Providence, Eleuthera, and on Amazon.com in Kindle and paperback. She can also be reached at tbethel@booksbybethel.com.

SCRIPTURES TO COMFORT AND ENCOURAGE

Below is a small selection of Bible verses to bring you comfort and encouragement. All verses are from the New Living Translation (NLT).

But don't be afraid of those who threaten you. For the time is coming when everything that is covered will be revealed, and all that is secret will be made known to all. Matthew 10:26.

Don't be afraid, for I am with you. Don't be discouraged, for I am your God. I will strengthen you and help you. I will hold you up with my victorious right hand. Isaiah 41:10.

So be strong and courageous! Do not be afraid and do not panic before them. For the Lord your God will personally go ahead of you. He will neither fail you nor abandon you. Deutoronmy 31:6.

Don't worry about anything; instead, pray about everything. Tell God what you need, and thank him for all he has done. Then you will experience God's peace, which exceeds anything we can understand. His peace will guard your hearts and minds as you live in Christ Jesus. Philippians 4:6-8.

Trust in the Lord with all your heart; do not depend on your own understanding. Seek his will in all you do, and he will show you which path to take. Proverbs 3: 5,6.

Study this Book of Instruction continually. Meditate on it day and night so you will be sure to obey everything written in it. Only then will you prosper and succeed in all you do. This is my command— be strong and courageous! Do not be afraid or discouraged. For the Lord your God is with you wherever you go. Joshua 1:8,9.

But when I am afraid, I will put my trust in you. I praise God for what he has promised. I trust in God, so why should I be afraid? What can mere mortals do to me? Psalm 56:3,4.

Search for the Lord and for his strength... 1 Chronicles 16:11.

The Lord is close to all who call on him, yes, to all who call on him in truth. He grants the desires of those who fear him; he hears their cries for help and rescues them. Psalm 145:18,19.

A final word: Be strong in the Lord and in his mighty power. Ephesians 6:10.

SCRIPTURES FOR PROTECTION

But the Lord is faithful; he will strengthen you and guard you from the evil one. 2 Thessalonians 3:3.

So humble yourselves before God. Resist the devil, and he will flee from you. James 4:7.

But in that coming day no weapon turned against you will succeed. You will silence every voice raised up to accuse you. These benefits are enjoyed by the servants of the Lord; their vindication will come from me. I, the Lord, have spoken! Isaiah 54:17.

A final word: Be strong in the Lord and in his mighty power. Put on all of God's armor so that you will be able to stand firm against all strategies of the devil. For we[a] are not fighting against flesh-and-blood enemies, but against evil rulers and authorities of the unseen world, against mighty powers in this dark world, and against evil spirits in the heavenly places. Therefore, put on every piece of God's armor so you will be able to resist the enemy in the time of evil. Then after the battle you will still be standing firm. Ephesians 6:10-13.

The righteous person faces many troubles, but the Lord comes to the rescue each time. Psalm 34:19.

O Lord, keep me out of the hands of the wicked. Protect me from those who are violent, for they are plotting against me. Psalm 140:4.

But you, O Lord, are a shield around me; you are my glory, the one who holds my head high. I cried out to the Lord, and he answered me from his holy mountain. I lay down and slept, yet I woke up in safety, for the Lord was watching over me. Psalm 3:3.

Look, I have given you authority over all the power of the enemy, and you can walk among snakes and scorpions and crush them. Nothing will injure you. Luke 10:19.

Yes, and the Lord will deliver me from every evil attack and will bring me safely into his heavenly Kingdom. All glory to God forever and ever! Amen. 2 Timothy 4:18.

Now may the God of peace make you holy in every way, and may your whole spirit and soul and body be kept blameless until our Lord Jesus Christ comes again. God will make this happen, for he who calls you is faithful. 1 Thessalonians 5:23-24.

For the angel of the Lord is a guard; he surrounds and defends all who fear him. Psalm 34: 7.

SECURE YOUR COPIES

We hope you have been encouraged and inspired by the stories shared in this book. If you have, contact our courageous overcomers to encourage them. We also invite you to send in your reviews.

Contact one of our contributing writers to secure additional copies of this book for your reading groups. If you are not in the Bahamas, you can order a paperback copy on Amazon.com.

Be blessed!

JOIN AN INSPIRATIONAL ANTHOLOGY

Are you a writer or someone with an empowering story to tell? Then perhaps being a part of an anthology is for you. For more information on how you can participate, visit us at:

www.InspirePublishing.org/multi-author-anthology.

Made in the USA
Columbia, SC
23 January 2025

52264573R00076